The Investor's Odyssey

The Investor's Odyssey

Resisting the Sirens and Playing the Long Game

Christopher W. Mayer

Partners Media

The Investor's Odyssey
Resisting the Sirens and Playing the Long Game

By Christopher W. Mayer

Library of Congress Control Number: 2026908077

ISBN: 979-8-9914735-0-7
1. Business & Economics—Investments & Securities—Stocks
2. Business & Economics—Personal Finance—Investing
3. Business & Economics—Entrepreneurship

Cover design by Yvonne Münzberg
Edited by Eddie Palmgren
Book design by Fifth Letter

Printed in the United States of America

Partners Media
158 West 75th Street, Suite 4B
New York, NY 10023

Dedicated to Charles T. "Chuck" Akre –
who helped teach me how to resist the Sirens
and play the long game.

TABLE OF CONTENTS

FOREWORD

Chuck Akre

Note by the author Chris Mayer: Chuck Akre is the founder of Akre Capital Management. The following foreword is an excerpt from his 2011 speech "An Investor's Odyssey: The Search for Outstanding Investments," given at the 8th Annual Value Investor Conference held in Omaha on the day before Berkshire Hathaway's annual shareholder meeting. His speech sets the tone and orientation for what follows in this book. I've learned a lot from Chuck over the years and he's had a big influence on how I think about investing. The excerpt is curated and used with permission. You can find the entire speech online.

MY CHAT TODAY IS CALLED "An Investor's Odyssey: The Search for Outstanding Investments." It's a loose summary of my experience in the investing business. I've gained enough weight and lost enough hair over the years to be able to allow me to write up some thoughts about investing, so today I'm going to share with you some of these thoughts, which collectively have added value in my career.

Many years ago when I started my investing career in Washington D.C., I was puzzling with several questions about investing, and mind you that I came into this with a BA degree in English Literature, having also been in a pre-med program, so I actually had a great many questions. Among the questions were, "What makes a good investor?" and more to the point, "What makes a good investment?"

Today we tell all of the clients in our firm that our primary goal is to compound their capital at an above-average rate while incurring a below-average level of risk. So I ask my friends: Which would you rather have, $750,000 today or the outcome of doubling a penny a day for 30 days. What's the value of compounding? Well, the answer in this case is simply astounding. Doubling a penny a day for 30 days gets you $10 million, $737,000, and change.

The reason why we use the notion of compounding our capital at above-average rates is that we can think of no better method of measuring the success of any business. Think for a moment about that, if you will. How else is someone able to judge the success of a business enterprise than through some measurement of the growth in real economic value?

Granted, we all know about the importance of customers and employees and community, and obviously they're important, but throughout my odyssey I've been trying to identify and measure financial success in a manner other than whether the share price rises or falls. In fact, in a private business one is not afforded the luxury of share price discovery, so some other method of measuring success must be present.

In our firm we use a visual construct of an early 20th century three-legged milking stool to represent the three things that we focus our attention on. The three legs are sturdier than four because they always present a steady surface on uneven ground.

Leg number one stands for the business model of the company. For us, it's important to understand just what it is about the model that causes the good returns. And what's the outlook? In our office we often say, "How wide and how long is the runway?"

The second leg of the stool is about the people in the business. We often ask ourselves whether they treat public shareholders as partners, even though they don't know them. My life experience teaches that once someone puts his hand in your pocket, he will do so again.

We refer to the third leg of the stool, which quite obviously gives it its stability, as the glue that holds the opportunity together. My next question, therefore, is: does an opportunity exist to reinvest all the excess cash generated by a business, allowing it to continue to earn these attractive above-average returns? My experience tells me that the reinvestment issue is perhaps the single most important issue facing any CEO today. As value can be added or subtracted quickly and permanently, this relates to both the skill of the manager and the nature of the business.

After we've identified a business that seems to pass the test regarding all three legs, we refer to it as our compounding machine. Our valuation discipline then comes into play. Here we simply describe it as unwillingness to pay too much.

Volatility is not part of our analysis of risk; rather we view it as an opportunity generator. The risk involved is the permanent loss of capital. To avoid that, we're watching for deterioration in any of the three legs of our stool. Is the economic moat drying up, are the managers behaving badly in some way, or is the reinvestment opportunity diminished or being abused?

You have to have your eyes open all the time. I have this motto, "In life as well as in business, which is every day, I'm lucky if I have learned something new, and I'm doubly lucky if it hasn't cost too much."

Now it's time to go fishing. The pond I want to fish in is the one where all the fish are of the high-return variety.

INTRODUCTION

Mapping Out the Odyssey

AS CHUCK AKRE ASKED in his speech, "What makes a good investor?" What does it mean to say someone is a good investor?

Before you answer, consider the following story.

I was sitting on a plane headed to Berkshire Hathaway's annual event in Omaha. I was in the first row after business class with an empty seat next to me. An apologetic flight attendant soon appeared leading an elderly woman who had been bumped from first class and seated her beside me.

My new seatmate and I got to chatting. It turns out that she was an investor in the original Buffett partnership (created in 1956). And when Buffett, in 1965, took control of Berkshire, she invested in that.

The lady told me stories about the early Berkshire meetings (She attended every one.) and how, back in the early days, the annual meeting consisted of only a handful of people who would meet for dinner. She was quite rich when I met her, as you might imagine, and lived in Nantucket. She told me that she gives a little bit of Berkshire stock to her grandchildren every year.

I thought, *this woman's track record as an investor is fantastic.* She made one move — buying Berkshire. And then she left it there for a long time. Would you say she is a good investor? Why, or why not? Is a good investor someone who can take apart a financial statement? Who knows a lot about markets and businesses and manages a lot of other people's money?

Or can a good investor simply be someone who saw a great opportunity, bought it, held it, and made a fortune? Her track record as an investor undoubtedly beats many money managers, including some of the all-time greats.

That woman who owned Berkshire all those years and moved to Nantucket didn't care at all about quarterly performance, what the Fed was doing, whether the S&P was in a flag-and-pennant chart formation, or a long list of other things people obsess over. She resisted those sirens, those calls to action, and played the long game instead.

What did the Fed do? Didn't matter.

What about economic analysis and predictions? Didn't matter.

What about interest rates and employment data? Didn't matter.

Is the market overvalued or not? Didn't matter.

None of it mattered, except to the talking heads and publishers who needed something to sell.

This woman's story contains a lot of wisdom. In a way, everything in this book unpacks her odyssey. Hers was an ideal investing journey, which we will map out.

Berkshire was a great investment choice. But there were (and are) many others out there. They share some traits, which we will explore. At a high level, all we need is a good business plus healthy dollops of patience.

Not everyone has the temperament or the patience to hold on to a stock for a couple of decades, although there are ways to cultivate these admirable virtues (which you will see later). To figure out how you want to invest, you must first get to know yourself. That is no easy task either. It takes time. And there will probably be some pain early on as you stumble around.

The journey never ends because you learn new things about yourself — your tendencies, weaknesses, and strengths — as you accumulate new experiences. That's part of the fun: learning and striving to improve. In the following pages, we will discuss this evolving process in great detail.

* * *

Good Investing Is Easy… Or Is It?

Our lady from Nantucket didn't seem to be trying very hard. After all, she bought one stock and held it. However, she is an exemplar in that way, and many investors would do well to emulate her rather than keep busy with activities that add nothing to their returns. Good investing like hers can seem effortless to the outside observer.

This reminds me of an investment speech titled "Trying Too Hard," by Dean Williams, a Senior Vice President of Batterymarch Financial Management. He gave the speech at Rockford College in the summer of 1981.

Williams's basic idea is that we investors are trying too hard to do well. And in that effort, we do all kinds of things that don't add to our returns. In fact, most of the things that we investors like to do work against us.

Williams tells the story of how he was working for an investment firm and had just completed what he thought was "some fancy footwork involving buying and selling a long list of stocks." Rather proud of what he'd done, he showed his list to the most senior member of the investment committee, who asked him, "Do you think you might be trying too hard?"

At the time, he thought the idea of "trying too hard" was absurd. Aren't you supposed to try hard? Over time, he came to see the older man's wisdom.

Most of Wall Street, and financial markets generally, promote activity. They want you to trade. They want you to "manage risk," "play trends," and "re-balance." All the usual buzzwords for activity.

In his speech, Williams asks us to reflect on the sobering idea that maybe our efforts don't have as much to do with our returns as we think. Of course, all is not lost. He makes some good recommendations. But before we get to those, let's consider a few points in his argument.

Williams highlights the distinction between Newtonian physics and quantum physics. In a Newtonian world, some laws govern physical events. Rational prediction is possible. Quantum physics, though, suggests we don't know nearly as much as we thought we did. Physical events seem to defy logical explanation in a quantum world. Even observing and measuring such events without changing them seems impossible.

Similarly, there is security analysis, and then there is what happens in the real world. "There's just too much evidence," Williams said, "that our knowledge of what governs financial and economic events isn't nearly what we thought it would be."

I am a softie for this kind of thing. I wrote a book about the numerous limitations of our knowledge titled *How Do You Know?* My answer was, "You don't know — not for sure. And you can't know — not nearly as much as you think you can. But to have an idea about these boundaries is the beginning of wisdom." I believe a great deal of the activity is based on the false idea that we know a lot more about how the world works and what's going to happen next than we do.

Not knowing where their boundaries of knowledge are leads people to spend a lot of time doing things they can't do well. Making predictions is number one on that list of things. Earnings, growth rates, interest rates, and so on. "You can be a successful investor without being a perpetual forecaster," Williams said. "I can tell you from personal experience that one of the most liberating experiences you can have is to be asked to go over your firm's economic outlook and to say, 'We don't have one.'"

As Williams recommends later in his speech, "Give life a try without forecasts. You might even decide, as I have, that a portfolio manager without a forecast is a little like a fish without a bicycle."

If you're not forecasting, what do you do? Monitor the business you own and how it creates value over time. Ditch the forecasts.

My second favorite recommendation from Williams's speech is:

"Respect the virtues of a simple investment plan."

We're easily fooled, but may be less fooled if we stick with simplicity. It's hard to argue with the simplicity of our lady from Nantucket.

It's human nature to be attracted to things that seem complex and deep. Williams cites a funny experiment in which an actor delivers lectures to educated audiences on game theory using a lot of "double talk, meaningless words, false logic, contradictory statements, irrelevant humor, and meaningless references to unrelated topics."

And yet ...he snows them all. The audience found the lectures to be both smart and clear. None of them realized they were pure nonsense. I suspect they allowed complexity to dazzle and lost their moorings in the simple.

Sadly, this carries over to investing. People tend to rate complex research higher than research that is simple and straightforward. 100-page slide decks impress; they get passed around a lot. People believe that the person who put that slide deck together must know something. They did a lot of work. But an easily grasped idea expressed on a single page with six bullet points is not so much. Yet, as Williams says, "Mastery often expresses itself in simplicity."

I have seen this happen at conferences, too, where a good speaker holds the audience spellbound with a lot of charts and a fantastic delivery. They invariably go over their allotted time, but no one seems to mind. I remember one episode distinctly because the speaker was discussing something I happened to know a lot about. I could see right through him; his knowledge was superficial at best and downright wrong in some respects. But people loved his talk.

Highfalutin language and masses of details may be a mask. Don't fall for it.

My third and last recommendation from Williams is that you should cultivate "a very special tolerance for the concept of 'nonsense.'" You've probably heard of the concept of the beginner's mind. You try not to label things so quickly. You try not to let your expertise cloud your ability to see new ideas and patterns. The more we think we know, the more our worldview shrinks if we're not careful.

As investors, we often seek the opinions of experts on a technology or industry. But sometimes, it's best to approach things from an outside perspective.

Experts work in well-worn grooves of thought. Rare is the person willing to step outside a settled consensus. Yet, that's where outperformance often lies. I am pretty sure that every investment advisor would have advised our lady from Nantucket to sell some Berkshire and diversify. She seemed to keep to a much simpler idea — she believed in Buffett. She kept up with him by attending the annual meetings. She liked what she heard, and the performance was good. So she left it alone.

In summary, investing is a peculiar activity. In most aspects of life, if you put a lot of effort into something, you expect to get better results. In investing, the link between effort and reward is tenuous and long-tailed. Our lady in Nantucket is a great example of what you can accomplish with a simple approach that does not appear to be trying too hard.

Sosnoff's Law

I love the simple, minimalist approach to investing. Ironically, it's a challenge to keep it simple because we get lost in details and things that seem important now, but fade away into irrelevance over the years.

On this point, I would like to bring in another investor who has significantly influenced my thinking, but is not well known, even within investing circles. He wrote a few books, which are now long out of print. To me, he represents the epitome of the minimalist approach.

Martin Sosnoff is his name. He grew up in the Bronx tenements and served in the Korean War. He started in the money management industry in the 1960s and retired in 2016. I love his books, especially *Humble on Wall Street* (1975) and *Silent Investor, Silent Loser* (1986).

Do I agree with everything in his books? No. But I like his

attitude — cynical, skeptical, and wise. He is old school. Investing with coffee stains, pipe smoke, and pencil on paper.

A big idea I absorbed from Sosnoff's books was the idea of money management as a minimalist art. In today's world, we are inundated with information and noise, and we rely too much on numbers, models, and forecasts. Sosnoff's position is a well-needed vaccine.

He scoffs at the easy analysis provided by spreadsheets that extrapolate numbers. They are often wrong, but provide numbing comfort in the face of inescapable uncertainty. The big money, Sosnoff maintains, comes from "hard decisions for which there is no ready arithmetic."

Some of the most essential elements of investing are things you can't put numbers on, such as assessing the competitive position of a business or the integrity of management. The best ideas are usually the simplest. (Our lady from Nantucket had one simple idea: buy and hold Berkshire.) The harder you work to justify an investment, the less likely such ideas seem to pay off. These are the nuts and bolts of the minimalist approach.

This leads us to Sosnoff's Law: "*The price of a stock varies inversely with the thickness of its research file.*" In other words, the stocks you spend the most time researching are the ones that tend to give you the most trouble and will drop the furthest. The thinnest files, where you tend to spend the least amount of time (because the idea is so simple and compelling), tend to be the ones that go up the most. When things are working, we spend less time on them. When a stock is not performing well, we spend more time on it, often trying to bolster our case for why we continue to hold on to it.

I have at times forgotten this rule, always to my regret. The more time I spend on an idea, the less likely it is to work. I have, at times, cut ideas from my portfolio simply because I found they absorbed too much time and took up too much mental energy. There was too much drama.

Simple is better than complex. Easy is better than complicated.

A thesis you can jot down on a hotel notepad is better than one that requires a spreadsheet. If owning the stock makes you feel smart, it probably won't work. (Now, there are investors who thrive on the complex and create tremendous value in extremely sticky situations. But our approach here is not that.)

Simpler also means the chances are better that you can hold on longer, because you've reduced the investment down to only the essentials. If you have a complex thesis that depends on many variables, you're less likely to hold it for the long haul because more can go wrong. But are these extra variables critical for the success of the investment? In most cases, the answer is no. Narrow your investment case to what is absolutely necessary for success, and discard the rest.

I spent a couple of hours with Sosnoff in the summer of 2015 at his office on Park Avenue in Manhattan. At the time, he had a new book called *Master Class for Investors: Stand Alone to Win Big*. He hadn't lost anything on his fastball:

> "I long for simplicity in my investment schemata. Thin files make me richer, when I go against the grain. Thick files adumbrate long-winded rationalizations for holding on to disappointing investments."

As I get older, I increasingly agree with Sosnoff's minimalist approach. I want to own good and well-managed assets acquired at a fair price and hold them for a long time.

The Investor's Odyssey

With this basic orientation in place, we are ready to map out how we can find success such as that found by our lady from Nantucket. Investing is akin to a long journey, one that will be filled with trials. A powerful metaphor for this adventure is Homer's *Odyssey*, created some 2,700 years ago.

You may recall a few elements of this grand story, which have become embedded in our culture. The hero, Odysseus, is trying to make his way home to his beloved wife, son, and kingdom in Ithaca after the Trojan war. On the course of his ten-year journey, he faces many obstacles, such as the sea monsters, Scylla and Charybdis, and the sorceress Circe. One of the most famous of these trials is his encounter with the Sirens.

The Sirens are often portrayed as having the head and upper bodies of women atop the bodies of birds. They live on an island and sing sweet songs to lure sailors to steer their ships onto the rocks. The heaps of bones on the coast attest to the danger of their charms and temptations.

Odysseus must resist the Sirens to reach his destination. So he plugs his crew's ears with beeswax and orders them to lash him to the mast. And they sail through.

In a similar way, we investors will be tempted by many Sirens on our journey. To ignore them and stay the course is difficult, but in the pages that follow, we will look at many simple tools and ideas — ways to plug your ears and lash yourself to your mast so you don't stray.

Think of the lady from Nantucket and all the Siren songs she must've heard along the way, tempting her to "take profits," "rebalance," or "diversify." Not to mention the endless pitches to invest in something better, especially when Berkshire went through rough patches (It was cut in half three times and once went nowhere for seven years).

In the next section, we're going to take a look at the kind of odyssey we can expect. It's going to be stormy seas full of perils.

TOP TAKEAWAYS

1. *The lady from Nantucket became wealthy by purchasing Berkshire Hathaway and holding it for decades.*

2. *Her track record as an investor was brilliant and beat most professional managers. Patience and simplicity paid off, big time.*

3. *Three recommendations from Dean Williams's speech "Trying Too Hard": avoid forecasts, have a simple investment plan, and think independently.*

4. *Sosnoff's Law: The stocks you spend the most time and effort on are the ones that tend to give you the most trouble.*

5. *The best investments are often super simple.*

6. *Be aware of siren songs and resist falling for them.*

CHAPTER 1

Through Scylla and Charybdis

EVERY LONG-TERM WINNER, sooner or later, brings you to the straits of Scylla and Charybdis. It's here where the seas get choppy and you are beset with dangers on both sides. Odysseus knew there was no easy way through, only painful acceptance that progress required exposure to such dangers. Riding a great compounder is the same.

The stock price will fall, often dramatically and sometimes quickly with no warning. During such times, you can easily lose sight of the horizon. But to earn extraordinary returns, you must do what Odysseus did: hold steady and trust that your vessel — the underlying returns of the business you bought — and your talented crew, will pull you through the dangers. (We will look at these elements as we go).

Steady at the Helm

So, we recognize stock prices are moody. What can help us deal with the psychological toll?

To start, I recommend against following the returns of your portfolio too closely. For example, I try not to log in to the account unless I know I want to do something. I don't want the daily blow-by-blow on prices. It's terrible for the investing psyche; it makes you impatient and causes you to lose perspective.

Those prices flashing before your eyes cry out for action. Feeding that into your brain every day (or worse, multiple times a day) invariably compresses timeframes and makes every day seem essential. Before you know it, you are one of those people who go around with explanations for why such-and-such stock was up (or down) that day. It seems like a recipe for madness.

I prefer to cultivate a general awareness of where prices are. But I admit I can't help myself, especially when there is a lot of movement — either up or down. I can't help but look.

And as much as I train myself to see price declines in my holdings as not necessarily bad, a part of me frets over them. After all, I run money and have to report to investors. I'd rather not have my most prominent position drop 20% in a month. (Or down 50% in three months, which happened to my holding Lumine in 2025). Even though time and time again, such drops turn out to be opportunities — and I know this. It's never so easy when you go through it.

As a practical matter, no one buys into every decline. At some point, you are full, or you run out of money. Then there is nothing to do but sit and wait.

Volatility Takes a Bite

Let's look back at a bout of price swings ("volatility" in finance lingo) from November 2021. It was an unusual month and a notable example of heightened uncertainty in the real world. The S&P 500 was barely down for the month. But most stocks were down quite a bit more. Smaller-cap stocks outside the S&P 500 fared even worse. A friend tipped me to something LRT Capital Management put out, which did a good job showing this.

LRT pointed out that while the S&P 500 Index was down only 4% from its all-time high, the Russell 2000, which comprises smaller-cap stocks, dropped 12%. However, the fuller decline was much greater than that. The big index received a boost from mega-cap tech shares, whose large market caps had a disproportionate impact on the Index.

LRT dug in and looked at all the stocks in the S&P 500 Index (which actually had 505 stocks). Here is what they found:

Decline from 52 week high of at least:

10%	317
15%	205
20%	130
25%	78
30%	43
50%	6

AVERAGE DECLINE:

-15.5%

More than half of all stocks in the Index were down by more than twice the drop in the Index itself. They also found that the percentage of stocks trading at their one-year lows was the highest since April 2020. LRT made everyone feel a bit better that month.

Charlie Bilello, who posts interesting lists on his Twitter (now X) account, shared this one on the last day of November 2021:

Charlie Bilello @charliebilello Nov 30

November Returns... Nasdaq 100 $QQQ: +2%

$PLTR: -20%, $PYPL: -21%, $BABA: -23%, $ZM: -23%, $ROKU: -25%, $HOOD: -26%, $DKNG: -26%, $PENN: -28%, $BYND: -29%, $TREE: -30%, $TDOC: -32%, $OPEN: -33%, $CLOV: -34%, $BMBL: -35%, $UPST: -36%, $SDC: -40%, $Z: -48%, $PTON: -52%, $CHGG: -53%, $STNE: -54%

I didn't own anything on this list, but some air escaped from the tires that month. Even so, drawdowns are part of investing, even for "boring" (stable) businesses. But it helps to review this point. Even great stocks have nasty, gut-wrenching declines. I think of the Bessembinder study, which reviewed the top 100 firms that created the most value and found this about their paths:

32.5%

Average loss of value in a drawdown in the same decade as spectacular success

10 MONTHS

Average duration of those drawdowns

Again, those were the best stocks.

I didn't do much that November in 2021. I dribbled in some cash on a few positions, but nothing major. That's as it should be because … nothing major happened. That month soon faded in memory like the many months before it. They all blur together and become part of the tapestry of your returns.

Sharpe & Sortino

Others navigate the mood swings of the market differently. For example, I read a thoughtful interview from 2021 with Gavin Baker of Atreides Management in the Graham & Doddsville newsletter.

In this interview, Baker says:

> "You sit in an ivory tower and think, 'Oh, all I care about are returns over five to 10 years, and I don't care about the path to get there. I don't care about volatility.' That is true in an idealistic sense — the most significant risk is always the permanent loss of capital. But your clients care about volatility ..."

I won't say, "I don't care about volatility." I'd rather have a smooth ride. Who wouldn't? But that's not realistic. I will say that I don't actively manage volatility. If you can't handle volatility, don't invest in stocks. (Many investors are surprised when stocks act like stocks. It's kind of like eating fish but trying to get rid of the fish taste. Might as well not eat fish).

What I found most interesting about the interview with Baker was its candid discussion of the differences between managing a portfolio as a professional and managing one's personal portfolio. (I no longer have a personal portfolio; it's in my fund.) At one point, he says, "Maximize your Sharpe and your Sortino ratios because that is your job as a professional investor. As an individual investor, you should not care at all about those ratios."

Hmm — I don't know. I don't know what my Sharpe and Sortino ratios are. Did Buffett and Munger ever know their Sharpe and Sortino ratios? Did the lady from Nantucket? I know she was not a professional, but does that matter? Baker chides "idealists" and "philosophers." As people say nowadays, "I feel seen!"

There are different ways to sail through the straits. However, I like to think I'm doing what is best in the long run for my capital and my partners' capital, and that I'm not making undue concessions just because I'm a professional investor.

Simple But Not Easy

Let's digest some more gut-wrenching drawdowns. To begin, I want to bring in a book titled *Simple But Not Easy* by Richard

Oldfield. Oldfield is the founder of Oldfield Partners, a London-based money management firm. His book is a memoir about his investing experiences and the lessons learned over 40 years. It's well-written and even funny in parts. And he gives some good advice in the service of sailing through volatility storms.

In one of his stories, he writes about a meeting with clients where Oldfield expresses the belief that investing in Russia is safer than investing in Coca-Cola, a seemingly outrageous thing to say. This was in May 1997. Coca-Cola, a staid blue chip, was trading for a pricey 42 times earnings. Russia, which he had just spent time visiting, was full of cheap stocks with higher growth rates.

In August 1998, both the Russian stock market and currency collapsed. In US dollar terms, the market fell by 90% in just a few months. Now, that's a severe drawdown.

Oldfield thinks that his quip about Coca-Cola vs. Russia might haunt him as the silliest thing he's ever said. (I can sympathize. I've done a lot of interviews and public speaking. And I can think of some things I've said that I wish I hadn't.)

But mark the sequel.

From the bottom in 1998, the Russian market doubled. Then it doubled again. And again. The Russian ruble also recovered. By the end of 2005, the Russian market was *18 times* what it was at the end of 1998. From May 1997, when Oldfield made his quip, the market was worth 3.7 times more.

Coca-Cola earnings grew 60% over that time. But the price-earnings ratio fell from 42 to 21. By the end of 2005, the stock price was 21% lower than it was in May 1997.

Lessons

"Safety … is not an absolute term," Oldfield writes. "It is a function of both the investor's time horizon and of the investment's volatility." Oldfield says you should hold stocks for at least five years. You get the most benefit by giving them time to work.

Another takeaway from the story is that you must learn not

to bail out on your investments when disaster strikes. Think about the situation afresh. There may be something you can salvage. As Oldfield writes, "After such a share price fall, the right answer, emotionally difficult as it is, may be to go back for more."

After the 1987 crash, Oldfield's firm decided to hold 40% of its assets in cash. They had a big-picture thesis about how the world had changed. They didn't think things would get better anytime soon.

Of course, they were completely wrong as the market recovered.

This experience leads to another good nugget. "Dogmatic large scale views of prospects for the world, or for markets in general, are as unwise as betting all one's chips on a single number in roulette."

A portfolio should consist of more than one big idea. If you think inflation is a threat, fine, but don't commit 100% of your portfolio to that view. You could be wrong. As an investor, you can't afford to be dogmatic.

As Oldfield's well-chosen title says, investing is simple, but not easy.

Drawdowns: A Key Feature of Big Winners

Oldfield's experience with Russia — and other examples we've mentioned to this point — show the importance of drawdowns. As I've said, drawdowns are part of the life of every investor. Invariably, if you own a stock for a long time, you will have to sit through several.

Ever since I wrote my book on 100-baggers, I've been intrigued — some say obsessed — with the price drops of even the best-performing stocks. I love to look back at these winners and see the depth and duration of these drawdowns. It's always somewhat surprising — and instructive.

What I found affirmed what Peter Lynch once said, "The real key to making money in stocks is not to get scared out of them."

Knowing this, you can be more circumspect about drops in your stocks. As long as the underlying business continues to perform within an acceptable band of expectations, you are probably better off staying put.

Let's look at two positions I owned and their drawdown histories. These are just for illustrative purposes. Not all companies recover from their drawdowns.

Dino Polska

Dino Polska, a Polish grocer, has been a great business. Between 2020 and 2023, Dino averaged a 30% return on its equity and reinvested all of its profits to open new stores. During this time period, the number of stores doubled.

In October 2023, the stock was down about 25% from its peak. It was the fourth drawdown of at least 20% in the last three years. And yet, if you just sat on it for all 3 years, you enjoyed an 18% annual return, or 64% in total.

The rational mind hunts for reasons for these declines. Our brains want a narrative. And so we find reasons, or make up reasons. But do they matter?

The latest drawdown in this example seemed sparked by an earnings report showing significantly slower growth than the same quarter a year ago. Should we give such weight to quarterly results? Rarely do they matter. It was not the first time Dino had a "soft" quarter. It won't be the last.

And yet, Dino was a rewarding investment. Again, an 18% annualized return over three years, despite four drawdowns of 20% or more. Experiences like these have reinforced the research I've done on drawdowns. They happen, and they should not cause you to panic.

Brown & Brown

Brown & Brown is an insurance broker based in Daytona, Florida. I have owned shares since the inception of my fund in January 2019. Until September 2023, the stock returned about 20% annually, or 141%. Yet, it was not a smooth ride. Take a look at the chart below.

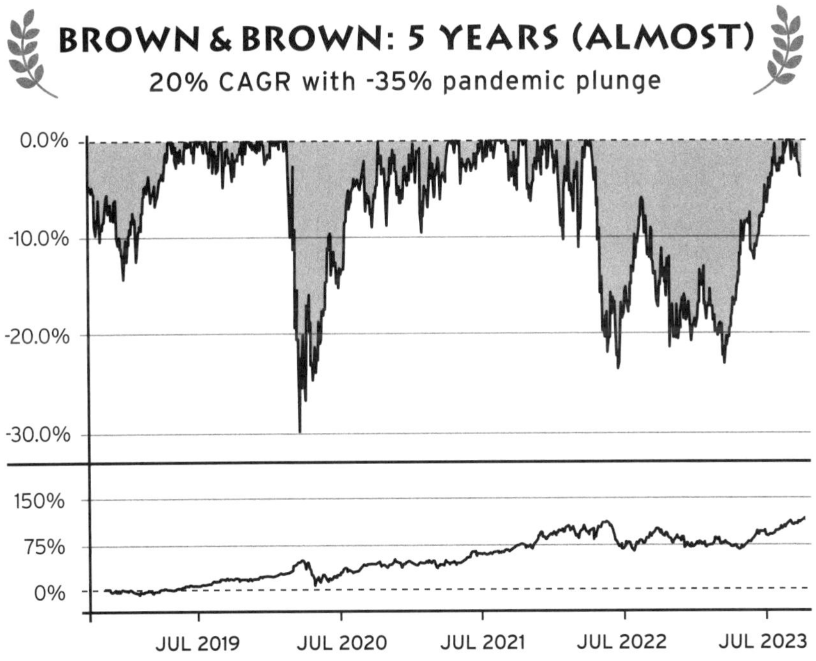

That giant crater is 2020, the year of the COVID-19 pandemic. The stock lost nearly 35% of its value, from peak to trough, in 2020. It took almost a year to return to the peak. Brown & Brown suffered a few more drops of more than 20%, including a 26% drawdown that lasted a year and a half.

It is one thing to say that stocks suffer declines and you have to sit through them. It is another thing actually to see it visually presented in this way, and yet another to experience them first-hand. I don't think most people quite appreciate how "normal" it is for winning stocks to have frequent and severe drawdowns. I want to emphasize again, these are high-performing stocks getting whacked.

For ease of reference, and for those future times when a stock you own suffers such a decline, I have compiled a handful of other examples of recent big winners and their drawdowns.

Study These Charts!

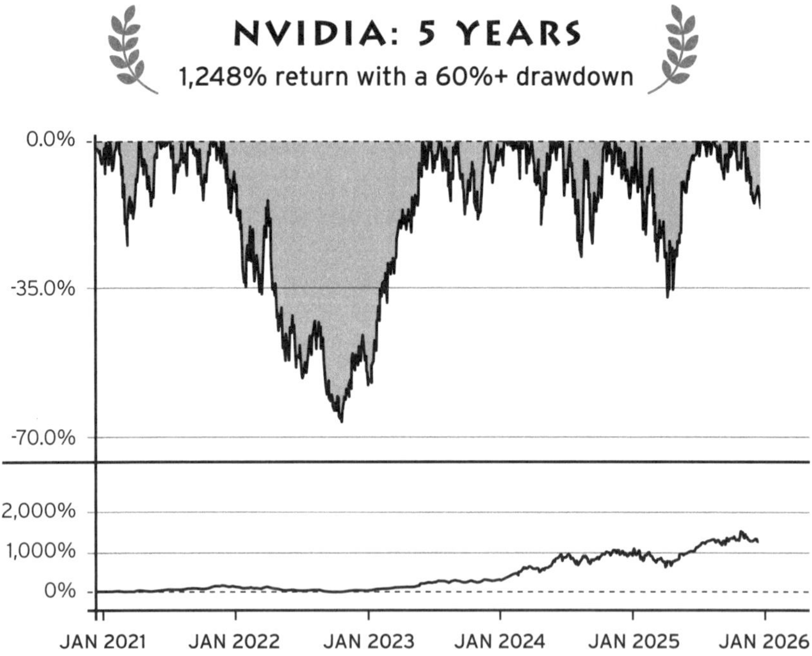

META: 10 YEARS

including a whopping 76% drawdown in 2022

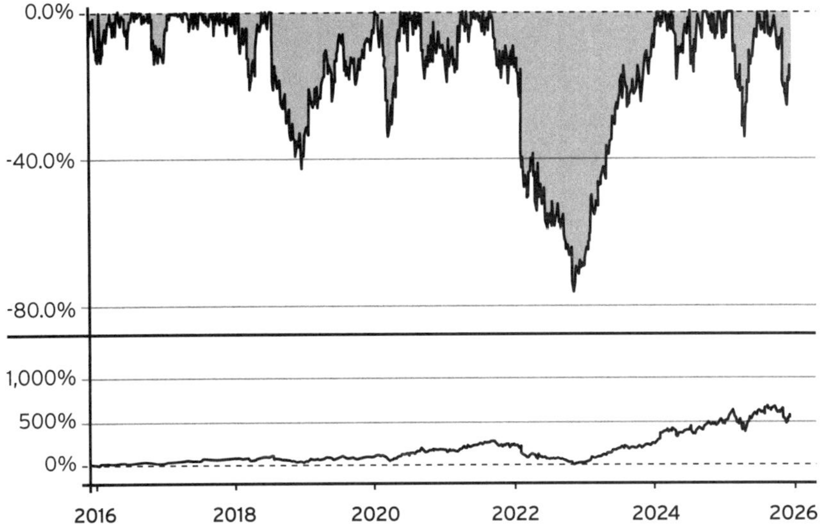

AMAZON: 20 YEARS

cut in half twice, several 30% drops, still returned 9,000%

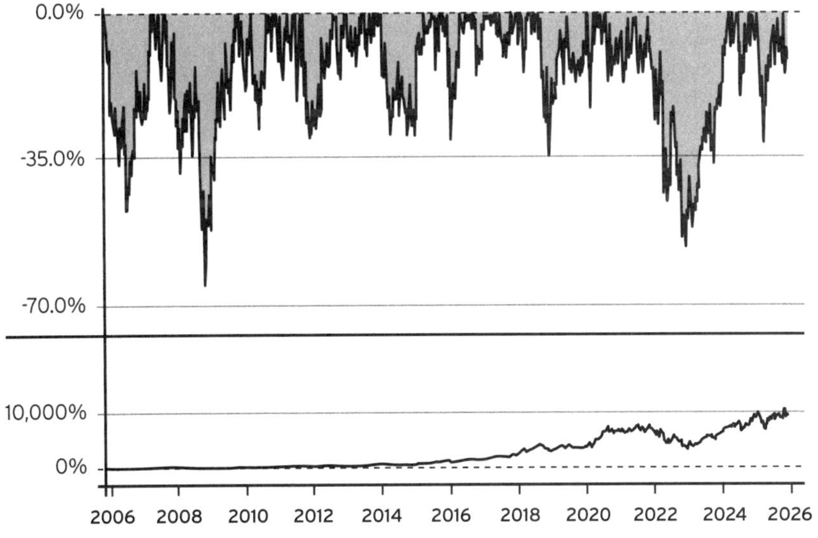

APPLE: 20 YEARS

"I have nothing to add," as Charlie Munger often said.

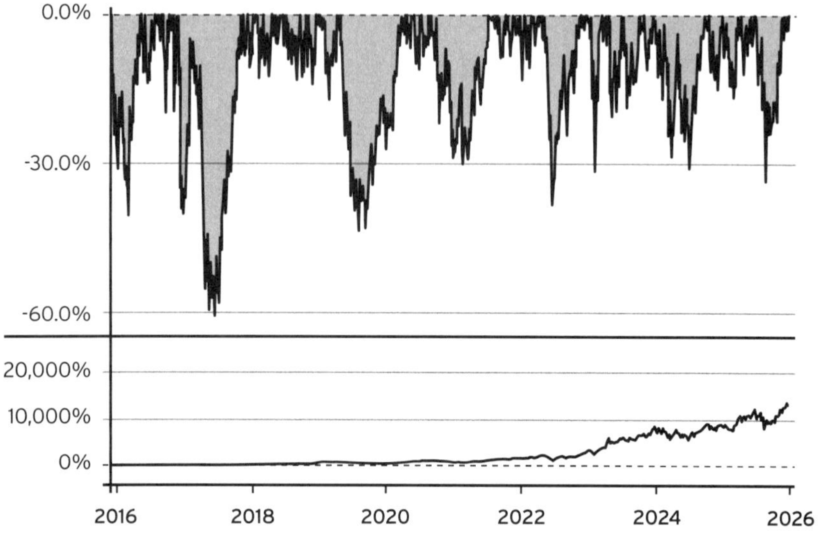

Peter Lynch's 21 Drawdowns

Not only do the best stocks suffer frequent and lengthy drawdowns, but the best investors also suffer drawdowns that would surprise most.

Peter Lynch, for example, had four severe drawdowns during his Hall of Fame run at Fidelity. Even though he returned a mind-boggling 29% annually, he had many setbacks during those years, including three of more than 20%, one of which was a hair-raising 42% drop in 1987. And this despite Lynch being highly diversified and having a high turnover rate in his portfolio throughout his career.

In summary, there is no defense against drawdowns if you are committed to a long-term, ownership-based approach to stocks. In fact, I would go so far as to say that the ability to sit through drawdowns with equanimity is a source of outperformance. It is a competitive advantage over those who can't. The ability to sit

PETER LYNCH

Number of Drawdowns While Running Magellan

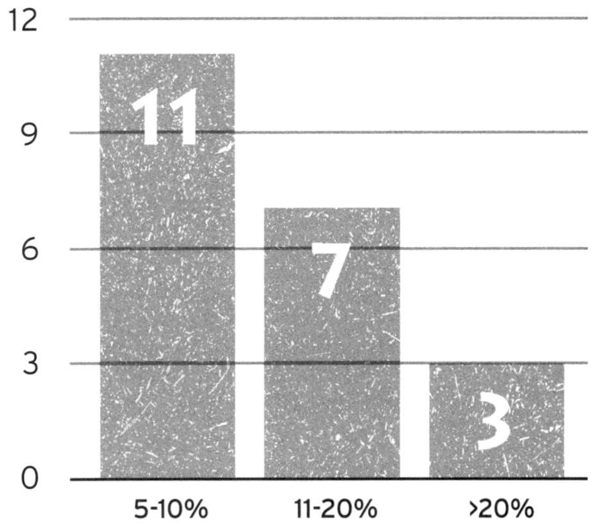

through drawdowns is the only path to enjoying those multi-baggers over time.

Financial History as Teacher

Let's come back to Charlie Munger. He furnishes a lot of grist for the investing mill. Munger said, "There is no better teacher than history in determining the future ... There are answers worth billions of dollars in a $30 history book."

Clearing old papers in my office, I came across several essays on the 1929 crash, well-marked with my pencil highlights. *The Journal of Portfolio Management* put together, in 1979, a 50-year retrospective titled "What Happened and Why?" Some of Wall Street's sharpest minds wrote pieces for the collection.

After re-reading a few, particularly given this discussion on drawdowns, I thought I'd share some interesting bits below on investing during a crash — in this case, one of the biggest in history.

Bernstein on Investing Through The Crash

Today, we know Peter Bernstein for his classic books, such as *Against the Gods: The Remarkable Story of Risk* and *Capital Ideas: The Improbable Origins of Modern Wall Street.* But in 1979, he hadn't written any of those yet. Remarkably, he was already 60 years old, a ripe age on Wall Street at the time.

Bernstein titled his essay in the retrospective collection "How I came to Be the Oldest Man Around." He writes he is virtually alone in his age cohort and knows almost no one 60 or older. Bernstein admits that age may not seem to have much to do with the crash, "but bear with me."

Bernstein says the crash acted as a herd-thinning event among Wall Streeters. After 1929, few young people decided to enter the investing business, creating a generation gap. The go-go market of the 1960s, Bernstein says, could only emerge when a fresh crew — lacking the painful memories of the '29 — replaced the banged-up and skeptical veterans.

It's an old idea — frothy bull markets run on the forgotten memories of old bear markets. Maybe. But Bernstein makes a more powerful point later in the same essay about the power of sticking to your stocks through thick and thin.

He believes in the old Wall Street adage that success comes not from "timing the market" but from "time in the market." Bernstein shows that even the Great Crash of 1929 failed to disprove this idea.

An investment in the Dow in 1924, held until the summer of 1936, meant you bought at ~100 and sold at ~160. Along the way, you earned $82 in dividends. "This meant you would have enjoyed a total annual return of 7.6% before taxes," Bernstein writes, "not including the reinvestment of dividends."

He also notes that the cost of living fell by around 20%, or nearly 2% per year. Not bad. And remember, you just sat on your hands the whole time. Bernstein plays with start/end times, but even if you held to 1939, when the market was less "ebullient," the return works out to 6% annually. "These returns are hardly anything to sniff at," Bernstein writes.

I agree with his message, but I will add that the ride to the destination was anything but smooth.

Historian Robert Sobel provides an example. He says, consider the investor who bought shares in Commercial Solvents, a thriving chemical company, in 1923 for $15 per share. By late 1932, the stock traded for $35 a share. Our investor has more than doubled. Sounds like a happy outcomc, right?

But, the stock traded for $1,400 in 1929. Now, how do you think you'd feel? A successful investor must be prepared to look foolish sometimes.

The Temptation of Trimming

So, since big drawdowns are common, the best strategy should be to secure profits when stocks soar to the sky, and then buy the dips?

Well ... yes, in theory. To give you a salt-stained case from reality, this is how I managed one of my most prominent positions during five years of ups and downs. I chose this example because the stock moved a lot in a relatively short period of time and is a good illustration of the principles we've covered. Don't assume this is a typical experience.

Topicus

Topicus is a spin-off from Constellation Software. I bought several more shares after the spin-off began trading in 2021. I intended to own it for at least a decade. The stock had a good shot of being a 5-10 bagger over its first decade as a public equity.

The stock dashed out of the gate. At its 52-week high in that first year, I was up over 120%. It zoomed to the top of my portfolio stack. That's a lot in a short amount of time. And it seemed the shares, as people like to say, "got ahead of the fundamentals."

So, trim or not?

TOPICUS: HYPOTHETICAL RETURNS

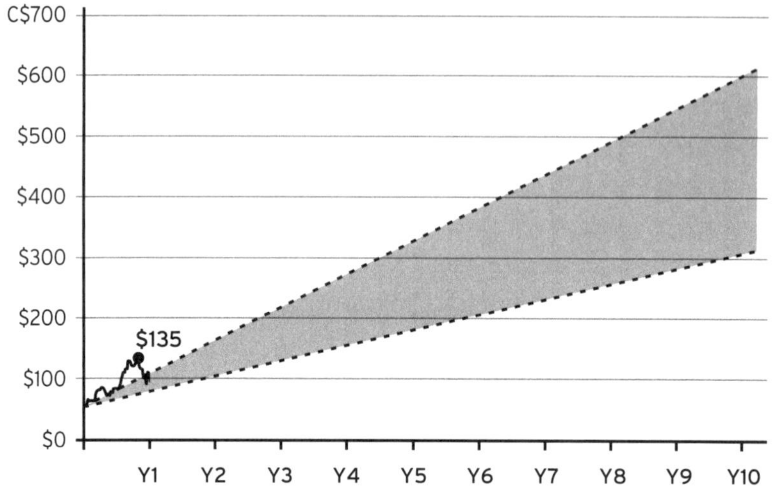

I chose not to. As a general rule, I don't like to trim. I'd rather allow the portfolio to become undiversified and unbalanced, which is a natural outcome of a healthy long-term orientation. Over time, certain positions are just going to get big. I think this is one of the paths to generating great overall returns in a portfolio. It's the path I've chosen to follow.

But this strategy has its pain points when a prominent position draws down. Naturally, people like to trim when a position gets large to lessen the pain.

Trimming, or trading around positions, can look smart and feel good, as I've mentioned. Shouldn't I trim when something becomes "expensive?" Shouldn't I put the money in something less expensive? Isn't that what "active managers" do?

If I were Superman, I could make such deft moves without error. However, in the real world, making this a practice leads to a dizzying chain of decisions that creates numerous opportunities for mistakes (besides making the tax authorities happy).

If I think Topicus has a good shot at being C$300-C$600 per

share in ten years, why trim at C$140, even if I think the stock is ahead of itself, so to speak? If I trim I face:

- **Fees.** Commission and taxes — a significant drag on performance over time. Most people don't realize how much better your replacement idea has to be to make a swap worth it. [See sidebar "How Good Does a Replacement Have to Be?"]
- **Reinvestment risk.** What should I do with the cash? When? Will that do better than leaving it in Topicus?
- **Execution risk.** Will I have the chance to buy back Topicus at a lower price? Would I take the chance? When? In my long experience, I am often better off just leaving it alone. If you have a long-term horizon, don't sell good businesses. As Marty Whitman used to say, "You make more money sitting on your ass."

HOW GOOD DOES A REPLACEMENT HAVE TO BE?

Suppose you own Stock A, currently worth $100,000. Your cost basis is $50,000 and the stock doubles. Your unrealized gain is $50,000. Assume the capital gains tax rate is 20%.

If you sell Stock A, you owe: $50,000 × 20% = $10,000 in taxes and have $90,000 to reinvest. That $10,000 is gone forever. It no longer compounds.

Now, let's compare two paths over the next **10 years.**

Option 1: Do Nothing

You keep Stock A and it compounds at 10% annually.

After 10 years, you have: $\$100{,}000 \times (1.10)^{10} \approx \$259{,}000$

No tax has been paid yet. The full $100,000 has been working for you the entire time.

Option 2: Switch to a "Better" Idea

You sell Stock A, pay the tax, and reinvest $90,000 into Stock B. Now, what return does Stock B need to match the $259,000 outcome?

Solve for *r*:

$$\$90{,}000 \times (1 + r)^{10} = \$259{,}000$$

That requires:

$$r \approx 11.2\% \text{ per year}$$

So, even though Stock A earns just 10%, your replacement investment must earn 11% *just to break even.*

That extra ~120 basis points per year is the *minimum hurdle* imposed by taxes alone. (Another way to think about it is that the return on your replacement has to be 12% better, per year, than the return on your existing investment).

And, of course, your new idea might be better.

This example only covers one swap. Imagine switching out four or five times over a 10-year period. It gets increasingly difficult to beat Stock A, which is humming along at 10% annually, tax-free.

If Stock A compounds at a higher rate, say 15% instead of 10%, the hurdle gets even higher, 16.2%. Again, just to break even on one swap.

Bottom line: Selling a good stock doesn't just require a better stock. It requires a *meaningfully* better idea. Taxes raise the bar more than most investors realize. (And in this case, we assumed no trading costs).

I would've sold some Topicus at C$140 per share if I were worried about quarterly performance, fixated on preserving my good returns for Q4 and a nice payday at year-end. But as an investor in my fund, is that what you want me to focus on?

This is a good test to see if I am doing what I have been promising. Am I focused on owning businesses that will create significant long-term value? Or am I playing the performance game by trying to trade stocks to outwit the market?

So, I held on to Topicus and was cut in half the following year. This was not pleasant, but I used the opportunity to increase my stake. Almost five years after the spin-off, the stock has compounded at about 15.3% annually (as of Jan 2, 2026). It's on pace for a sevenfold return in ten years (and 53x in twenty years). Of course, there are no guarantees and time will tell if Topicus works out or not. I expect more peaks and valleys along the way. Look me up in a decade, and let's see how it panned out.

Lashing Yourself to the Mast

One way to avoid touching your stocks is to embrace the coffee can idea. Selectively fill a jar, close the lid, and leave it be. Whatever happens in the can, stays in the can. This is similar to what Odysseus did when he asked his men to tie him to the mast.

Robert Kirby, who managed money for the Capital Group, was the first investor to use the coffee can idea. He wrote about it in 1984. In today's world, imagine being banned from your broker account for 10 years. What happens, then, is that you can't trim a position where you sell some of your stock because it seems to be "getting ahead of itself" or "it looks expensive," but keep the rest.

It's funny how people can be so confident making these frequent judgments of pruning their holdings, because perhaps the greatest investor of all time, Warren Buffett, was not.

During the 1997 shareholder meeting, Buffett mentioned how Coca-Cola and Gillette were wonderful businesses. There is always a risk, Buffett noted, even with great businesses such as these, you might pay a price where it will take a few years for the business to catch-up with the stock. He said,

"The stock can get ahead of the business. *And I don't know where that point is with those companies or any other companies.*" [my emphasis]. Now, that's a huge statement. Buffett was careful to say this doesn't mean you can pay any price. He tries to buy stocks cheap, but once he owns a wonderful business, he's unlikely to sell it.

So, next time you find yourself saying "the stock is getting ahead of itself," you might pause to add humility to that statement. If you already own it, and it's truly a great business, you are probably better off just holding.

In the following chapter, we will tune in to more of the sweet Siren songs.

TOP TAKEAWAYS

1. *Sail smoother: Don't follow the returns of your portfolio too closely.*
2. *The volatility in November 2021 seemed important at the time, but soon faded in memory like the many months before it.*
3. *Care about volatility, but don't actively manage it. (Don't eat fish if you don't like the taste of fish. Don't invest in stocks if you don't like the behavior of stocks.)*
4. *Investing is simple but not easy.*

5. *Russia beat Coke (at least for some time): Hold stocks for at least five years and don't mindlessly bail out when disaster strikes. Think about the situation afresh.*

6. *Investors can't afford to be dogmatic. Don't commit 100% of your portfolio to one big idea.*

7. *Even the best performing stocks and fund managers suffer dramatic and severe drawdowns.*

8. *A successful investor must be prepared to look foolish sometimes.*

9. *Trimming often costs more than we might think.*

CHAPTER 2

Resisting the Sirens

TO RIDE BIG WINNERS over the long haul, we need to stay focused on the things that matter. But there are plenty of distractions (those Sirens!). I once hosted a call with my investors and included an appendix titled "Interesting charts to consider*." The asterisk referred to a remark at the bottom: "But at the end of the day, [they] may not be that important."

The charts referred to "big picture" concerns — recent talk then was of inflation, rising interest rates, taxes, etc. All the usual macro concerns that people had at the moment ... I felt obligated to at least comment on these concerns. But I also felt compelled to say these macro concerns would not matter over the long-term.

The table on the following pages spans everything from trade wars to the end of quantitative easing, from the "fiscal cliff" to a Eurozone crisis.

What should strike anyone looking at this table is how none mattered to the long-term owner of publicly traded businesses. You could've slept through the whole thing. And your investments would've been acceptable.

What's in the headlines today seems so essential now, and then seems quaint a few years (or quarters) later. It is a mistake to adjust your portfolio based on these momentary concerns — if you're interested in nabbing those wonderful multi-baggers.

Multi-baggers need time to come to fruition. You won't get there trying to trade around recent events. You'll need to own great businesses and let them run on their own. Below is a short story to give you some perspective.

The Follies of Forecasting

Arthur Zeikel had a long and varied career on Wall Street, including a stint as president of Merrill Lynch. In an essay titled "After 50 years, Nothing New, Nor Likely," he targets economic and market forecasting — how errant they are and how investors rely too heavily on them. Most forecasting, he says, is just the extrapolation of current trends.

Zeikel draws a funny example from the author Shepherd Mead. The forecast involved pollution trends in New York City c. 1850. The primary sources of pollution were chewing tobacco and horse manure. The first sat half an inch thick in the gutters. And the latter half was an inch thick in the middle of the street. A little forecasting magic — extrapolation — put the depths at two inches by 1880 and 170 feet by 1970. Gosh, what a disaster!

Of course, such forecasts forget how people react and change their behavior. People did something about it once the spit and manure reached a certain level. Cigarettes and automobiles soon replaced chewing tobacco and horses.

It's an obvious lesson, but are investors committing the same mistakes in different industries today? Will oil surpluses last forever? Will AI infrastructure grow forever?

Zeikel ends with a nice bit of wisdom:

> "Investors must also appreciate that there is a pattern to events, but no pattern is perpetual. The more widely held the belief in the persistence of a pattern, the less likely it is to continue. **Investors frequently make too heavy a commitment to the configuration of trends already discerned.**" [bold added]

The Horse Story

What else can help you stay the course as a long-term business owner? And what Siren songs should you avoid? Let's begin with

S&P 500 CORRECTIONS

>5% since March 2009 low (as of April 7, 2025)

Correction Period	# Days	S&P High	S&P Low	% Decline
2025: Feb 19 - Apr 7*	**47**	**6147**	**4835**	**-21.3**
2024: Jul 16 - Aug 5	20	5670	5119	-9.7
2024: Mar 28 - Apr 19	22	5265	4954	-5.9
2022: Jan 4 - Oct 13	**282**	**4819**	**3492**	**-27.5**
2021: Nov 22 - Dec 3	11	4744	4495	-5.2
2021: Sep 2 - Oct 4	32	4546	4279	-5.9
2021: Feb 16 - Mar 4	16	3950	3723	-5.7
2020: Sep 2 - Sep 24	22	3588	3209	-10.6
2020: Feb 19 - Mar 23	**33**	**3394**	**2192**	**-35.4**
2019: Jul 26 - Aug 5	10	3028	2822	-6.8
2019: May 1 - Jun 3	33	2954	2729	-7.6
2018: Sep 21 - Dec 26	**96**	**2941**	**2347**	**-20.2**
2018: Jan 26 - Feb 9	14	2873	2533	-11.8
2016: Aug 15 - Nov 4	81	2194	2084	-5.0
2015/16: May 20 - Feb 11	267	2135	1810	-15.2
2014/15: Dec 29 - Feb 2	35	2094	1981	-5.4
2014: Dec 5 - Dec 16	11	2079	1973	-5.1
2014: Sep 19 - Oct 15	26	2019	1821	-9.8
2014: Jan 15 - Feb 5	21	1851	1738	-6.1
2013: May 22 - Jun 24	33	1687	1560	-7.5
2012: Sep 14 - Nov 16	63	1475	1343	-8.9
2012: Apr 2 - Jun 4	63	1422	1267	-10.9
2011: May 2 - Oct 4	**155**	**1371**	**1075**	**-21.6**
2011: Feb 18 - Mar 16	26	1344	1249	-7.1
2010: Apr 26 - Jul 1	66	1220	1011	-17.1
2010: Jan 19 - Feb 5	17	1150	1045	-9.2
2009: Oct 21 - Nov 2	12	1101	1029	-6.5
2009: Sep 23 - Oct 2	9	1080	1020	-5.6
2009: Jun 11 - Jul 7	26	956	869	-9.1
2009: May 8 - 15	7	930	879	-5.5
Median	**26**			**-7.6%**

"Stocks Fall On..."	*Source: Charlie Bilello*
Tariffs, Trade Wars and Global Recession Fears	
Recession Fears, Fed Behind Curve, Nikkei Crash	
Stubborn Inflation, Fed Pushing Back Rate Cuts, Iran/Israel Conflict	
Inflation, Rising Rates/Fed Tightening, Russia/Ukraine War, Recession Fears	
Covid Omicron Variant, Fed Taper Fears	
China Contagion Fears, Fed Taper Fears, Covid Delta Variant	
Inflation Fears, Rising Rates	
Coronavirus, No New Stimulus Deal, Election Fears	
Coronavirus, Global Depression Fears	
Trade War, Tariffs, Yuan Devaluation, Recession Fears	
Trade War, Tariffs, Inverted Yield Curve, Global Slowdown/Recession Fears	
Rising Rates, China Slowdown, Trade War/Tariffs, Housing Slowdown	
Inflation Fears, Rising Rates	
Election Fears/Concerns/Jitters	
Greece Default, China Stock Crash, EM Currencies, Falling Oil, North Korea	
Falling Oil, Strong Dollar, Weak Earnings	
Falling Oil, Strong Dollar	
Ebola, Global Growth Fears, Falling Oil	
Fed Taper, European Deflation Fears, EM Currency Turmoil	
Fed Taper Fears	
Fiscal Cliff Concerns, Obama's Re-Election	
Europe's Debt Crisis	
Europe's Debt Crisis, Double-Dip Recession Fears, US Debt Downgrade	
Libyan Civil War, Japan Earthquake/Nuclear Disaster	
Europe's Debt Crisis, Flash Crash, Growth Concerns	
China's Lending Curbs, Obama Bank Regulation Plan	
Worries About The Recovery	
Worries About The Recovery	
World Bank Neg Growth Forecast; Fears Market Is Ahead Of Recovery	
Worries That Market Has Gotten Ahead Of Itself	

a parable about a farmer.

A friend and I often invoke this story, which we call the "horse story." At a recent lunch, we agreed, "Everything is the horse story." I first read it in *Tao: The Watercourse Way,* a book by Alan Watts (1915-1973), which is a retelling of an old taoist tale from the 2nd century BC. Below is my rendition of the story.

The parable is about a farmer. One day, the farmer forgets to latch the barn door, and his horse escapes.

"That's bad news," his neighbors tell him.

But the farmer is more circumspect. "Maybe," he says.

The next day, the horse returns, accompanied by several other wild horses.

"Wow, that's great," the neighbors say.

"Maybe," says the farmer.

The next day, the farmer's son breaks his leg after being thrown by one of the new horses.

"That's rotten luck," the neighbors say.

"Maybe," says the farmer.

The next day, a war occurs, and men come to the village to draft soldiers. The farmer's son does not have to go.

"What good luck," the neighbors say.

"Maybe," says the farmer.

And so it goes.

"Bad" news may lead to a "good" outcome. And vice versa. I use quotation marks because I agree with Kurt Vonnegut, who said, "The truth is, we know so little about life, we don't really know what the good news is and what the bad news is."

We all have stories of apparent early setbacks with a stock where, in the long term, things worked out quite well. Or vice versa, when our first earnings report with the stock looked great, the stock popped, and we wound up losing money in the long term. It's the horse story.

You can relate (almost) everything that happens to the horse story. It may be beneficial to remember that when war and macroeconomic concerns drive stock prices. It keeps me more careful about things that seem "good" or "bad."

I try not to use those words. The market has no "good" or "bad" days. It depends on how you frame it.

This reminds me of something Buffett wrote years ago along similar lines. When you read headlines that discuss the decline of the stock market as a bad thing, you should mentally edit them to say, "Disinvestors lose as market falls, but investors gain." Though writers often forget this truism, there is a buyer for every seller, and what hurts one necessarily helps the other. (As they say in golf matches, "Every putt makes someone happy.")

In this section, we'll look at a variety of tools and ways that can help you lengthen your investing timeframe. Let's start with some things you should *not* do.

Don't Do These 5 Things

For inspiration, we turn to Paul Watzlawick (1921-2007), a psychologist, philosopher, and wise egg.

Watzlawick once wrote a book that turned the search for happiness on its head. Instead of writing a book on how to be happy, he wrote a book on how to be unhappy:

> "Our world, drowning as it is in a tidal wave of 'how to' instructions for the attainment of happiness, must no longer be deprived of a life-saver for those in pursuit of unhappiness...
>
> The number of persons talented enough to create their own hell may seem relatively large. But many more need help and encouragement. This little book is dedicated to them as an introductory text and a guideline."

The title of that book is *The Situation is Hopeless But Not Serious: The Pursuit of Unhappiness.* He writes about how people can make themselves unhappy, drawing on psychological research and his personal experience.

For example, glorifying the past at the expense of the present. (Things were always better in the old days.), thinking you will be happier after you attain something or another (leads to a regular diet of disappointment), or ignoring the power of self-fulfilling prophecies. "Self-fulfilling prophecies," he writes, "have a truly magical, 'reality'-creating effect and are thus of the utmost importance for our subject."

This latter point reminds me of a golf coach I had, who tolerated no negative thinking. If, for instance, you voice some concern about a sand trap in front of you, he'd say, "Bad attitude!"

Don't think about the sand. Think about putting the ball on the green. It's amazing how this works. I can tell you from experience that good things happen when you think good thoughts. Good investing, like good golf, starts with a proper mindset.

All this gets to the question of how you can you make yourself unhappy as an investor.

Here are five ideas, though I'm sure you can add to the list:

1. Watch stock prices during the day – and check in frequently

This is the worst! Everybody thinks they are immune to the Siren-like power of those blinking stock prices. You are not. I was glued to my computer screen when I started my fund in January 2019. I couldn't help it. I was putting money to work and eager to get off to a good start. It was awful. I'd feel tired at the end of the day. I quickly cut that out.

It's funny how watching prices magnifies their perceived moves. A stock moves 3%, which seems like a lot when you are watching it. Of course, over the long term, it doesn't mean anything.

Staring at your portfolio (especially when the market is open) might trigger a bias toward anchoring on certain round numbers, which become Siren songs themselves. Here are some common tunes to watch out for:

- "My weighted average cost per share is 105, but I want to get it down to 100."

- "My holding of stock X is worth $18,438, I want to round it off to $20,000."
- "I currently own 9,288 shares in stock X, but I want to own 10,000 shares."

These examples sound harmless, but they're irrational and they take your focus away from where it should be. I hear people talk like this, and not only retail investors.

Of course it's okay to *prefer* round numbers, the problem is if the desire to reach them impacts your investment decisions.

How can we resist the allure of round numbers, and what to do instead of checking stock prices?

- Remember that stocks don't care what you paid for them. Look forward.
- Think in terms of "percent of the portfolio" – the exact amount of dollars or number of shares doesn't matter.
- Put your attention on what you own, as a business. Try to understand these assets better – how they create value, how to think about what they are worth, etc.
- Always look for new investment ideas. The hunt is part of the fun. This is best done logged out from your broker account.

In general, I try to disentangle myself from the usually meaningless daily drama of the stock market. There are so many better things to do (like reading books, as you're doing now).

2. Watch financial coverage on TV or online

This is related to watching stock prices too closely. The problem with *all* media is that they aim to put on a show daily. Naturally, this means they must regularly make tornadoes out of zephyrs and floods out of spring showers.

As Louis Lowenstein put it, "One would think that something important is happening every day. ... The subliminal message is that you can't afford to relax, even for a moment." This is from his book *What's Wrong with Wall Street,* a forgotten classic. You probably know Roger Lowenstein, who wrote the famous biography of Warren Buffett, among other things. Louis is his dad.

The media focuses on many things that don't matter much to a long-term investor: the roll call of economic reports, the guesses of forecasters and economists. Upgrades and downgrades. Quarterly earnings beats and misses. If you want to be unhappy, pay attention to all that and try to invest well.

3. Look at all the top-performing stocks you don't own

Another way to get miserable is to regularly check the list of best-performing stocks year-to-date and see all you're missing.

Related to this, constantly consider how many investors are more knowledgeable and experienced than you are. This is guaranteed to cause you unhappiness. Read the quarterly letters of other investors and focus on their performance; there are always individuals who appear to be outperforming you.

There will always be somebody "better." And there are always stocks that will be moving faster than yours. So what. That's life. Stay with your game. Stick with what you do well. Trust in your process, and the results will come. If you try to play catch-up or be someone you are not, that's a path to misery.

4. Agonize over stocks you didn't buy but wish you did

Go through your watch list and look at all the stocks you didn't buy that went up the most. This is a great way to ruin an afternoon. My friends tend to do this. "Man, did you see XYZ? It's up 30% since we talked about it in January!"

Now, there is nothing wrong with learning from a stock you missed. But learn your lesson and move on. It does no good to stew over things you can't change.

5. Focus on what "should" happen

If you want to be unhappy, think about how the world "should" work. Write investment reports like "the market should value this company at 20x earnings, not 12." Say things like, "The market should go down because it's over-valued according to such and such." You get the idea.

The world doesn't need to follow any of your "shoulds." The sooner you realize that, the happier you'll be.

Watzlawick's book makes this point. He writes that a happier person shrugs and gets on with life, accepting that things won't work as they think they should. By contrast, the unhappy person constantly battles the world because it's not as it "should" be.

In investing terms, this translates into accepting that you could be wrong, being willing to revisit assumptions, etc.

Another way we can go wrong is by paying attention to surveys. In the financial world, there are various surveys conducted for consumer confidence, investor bullishness and bearishness, and more. Let's think about surveys for a minute.

Don't Rely on Surveys

In one of his comedy shows, Jerry Seinfeld talks about a survey that says public speaking is everyone's number-one fear. Not death, which is number two. Public speaking is number one. And the punchline is, to the average person attending a funeral, they feel they'd be better off in the casket than giving the eulogy.

Surveys are tricky things. We take what they say but rarely consider the knowledge of the people surveyed.

Author Neil Postman gives us a funny example, though a bit dated (from the 1980s). A survey indicated that 72% of Americans believed we should withdraw economic aid from Nicaragua.

Is that meaningful?

Postman urges us to consider that 28% of people surveyed thought Nicaragua was in central Asia. Another 18% thought it was an island near New Zealand. And 27% thought that "Africans should help themselves," obviously confusing Nigeria with Nicaragua. 61% didn't know that the US gave economic aid to Nicaragua, and 23% didn't know what economic aid means. As Postman put it, "If our pollsters were inclined to provide such information alongside their polls, perhaps the prestige and power of polling would be considerably reduced."

Don't Rely on the Media

Postman wrote a lot of what you might call cultural criticism. He was popular in the 1980s and 1990s. In particular, he focused on studying media and its effects on how we perceive the world. In his view, the effects were primarily adverse. These are great insights for long-term investors.

I recommend two books in particular: *Amusing Ourselves to Death* and *Technopoly.* One significant and profound thought ties these books together: the medium regulates and dictates its content. As Marshall McLuhan put it, "The medium is the message."

So what does this mean? Postman says to think about smoke signals. You can convey various messages using smoke signals, but can't express ideas about the nature of existence, right? You cannot use smoke signals to do philosophy, as Postman says. Its form excludes such content.

Likewise, TV, X (formerly Twitter), email, and other platforms all make specific demands on what and how people can discuss things. That's the meat of the idea.

In *Amusing Ourselves to Death,* published in 1985, Postman discusses television's impact and how it demands certain content. However, his insights can readily be applied to the Internet and social media.

Examine the media's influence on the US presidential election. Today's landscape demands a personality with a good command of TV and other media outlets. Getting elected today requires a different set of skills than it did years ago. It is hard to imagine some past presidents getting elected today. Lincoln? Most people never saw him, not even his picture, or heard his voice. Consider how different that is from what it is now.

And think about what media saturation does to our world of investing. How does a 24/7 news culture and social media impact the role of a CEO and the skill set required? What is rewarded, and what is punished? As Postman says, might it be that we give undeserved authority and prestige to those who have media skills over those who do not?

What about the nature of being an investor? What does the media demand of a "good" investor now? What does the media push us to do? Not do?

I don't have fully formed answers, but as Postman says, asking the question breaks the spell the media can cast over our thinking.

Postman wrote another book with Steve Powers, a TV anchor, called *How to Watch TV News*. In it, he suggests "what you can do."

I've taken his ideas, which apply to TV, and expanded them to include media in general (also financial media). So here are six suggestions:

1. When you encounter any media, you must start with a firm idea of what is essential

You will be endlessly manipulated if you have no clear sense of how to evaluate news or understand what is essential. Other people will dictate to you what they think is important. And really, it's not what they think is important; it's what they think is most interesting, controversial, etc. A journalist's goal is not to tell you what's essential … but to tell you a story they think you will want to read or see.

2. Keep in mind that it is a *show*

Media outlets of all kinds want eyeballs and want to sell advertising or get subscribers. To achieve this, they employ all the elements of show business to make it compelling.

This may seem simple, but it also applies to the Internet. The show must go on, and they want you in the audience.

3. Never underestimate the power of commercials

Postman: "Commercials are not fluff. Commercials tell us a lot about our culture. It can be a rich source of information about fears and motivations."

I differ a bit here. I look at commercials almost like magical spells that try to get you to do things. Advertising has become very sophisticated. Advertisers know how to push your buttons. (The comedian Bill Hicks used to refer to people in advertising as "Satan's little helpers.") I avoid commercials as much as possible.

4. Pay attention to language

Language is never neutral, and no one can be impartial.

For example, how you phrase or structure questions dramatically influences the kind of answers you get. Questions can never be unbiased. There is always a person asking the question. And there are always ways to ask the same question differently, vastly changing the odds of getting a specific answer.

A joke Postman tells makes this point. Two priests who were unsure whether it was permissible to smoke and pray at the same time wrote to the Pope for a definitive answer.

One priest asked, "Is it permissible to smoke while praying?" He was told it was not since prayer should be the focus of one's whole attention.

The other priest asked, "Is it permissible to pray while smoking?" He was told it is, since praying is always appropriate.

5. Reduce your intake of media by at least a third

You'll be less prone to its effects if you consume less media. There is nothing much more to it than that. But it's hard to do if you feel like you will miss out on something important.

Years ago, I cut back on my media consumption. I read three newspapers daily, but I cut that back to one, and eventually, none. I also canceled a bunch of financial magazines and publications. I don't feel like I've missed a thing.

If it's essential, you'll hear about it anyway. In the meantime, you'll have replaced media consumption with something better. Perhaps you'll read more about businesses, pick up an insightful biography, or read history.

6. Reduce by one-third the number of opinions you feel obligated to have

This is my favorite.

Postman writes that one reason many people are addicted to watching news is that they feel pressured to have an opinion about almost everything. College-educated, middle-class people seem especially burdened by an unrealistic and slightly ridiculous obligation to have a ready-made opinion.

Consider the absurd questions: What do you think about immigration policy, foreign policy, oil prices, or the next election?

Discover the liberating feeling of saying, "I have no opinion on this since I know practically nothing about it."

So, that's that. While the above may sound negative about the media, I realize there are benefits.

For example, I have a love-hate for X. On the one hand, it's a great marketing tool, and I get interesting stuff from certain people on X.

On the other hand, it can be a real time sink. I'll go through my feed and then realize an hour has passed and I've accomplished nothing. It's like junk food for the brain. I've cut way back on X to the point where I'm barely on it anymore. I don't miss it at all.

You are what you pay attention to. It's kind of like you are what you eat — if you spend hours on Facebook or X, cruising the internet, or watching videos, all those things become a part of you. So, consider what you choose to give your attention to. Your mind is like a garden. Put good things in it and take care of it, and you'll get better results.

Hold Fast: Phelps's Table

So what to do instead of watching tickers and the latest drama? Here's a great practice, and one I use, which should help you hold on to your stocks longer.

It comes straight from Thomas Phelps's 1972 classic, *100 to 1 in the Stock Market.* Here is what Phelps did in his book: He created a table with some basic financials of Pfizer over the previous 20 years. (See the table on the following page.)

It's fundamental, simple stuff. (Return on equity (ROE) is a basic measure of capital efficiency. We'll get to why capital efficiency is important in later chapters). And then Phelps asks "Would a businessman seeing only those figures have been jumping in and out of the stock?"

And he answers: "I doubt it."

I agree. Just look at those financials. That's a healthy business. And if you held on for 20 years, you were up something like 25x, excluding dividends.

But how many people held on for that 25-bagger? Probably not many. As Phelps writes, the financial industry won't let you. The industry conditions you to measure performance using quarterly or annual *stock prices.*

You rarely see anyone print their portfolio results by showing you anything like this table. You don't see anyone in their quarterly letter show you financial snapshots of the businesses in the portfolio or track their progress for you like this. No, you see them write about stock prices being up this or down that.

People obsess over stock prices.

And if you look at stock prices, you get a different picture. For Pfizer, there were the usual peaks and valleys, plus a five-year stretch where Pfizer trailed the market. And because so many people, in Phelps's words, have been "sold on the nonsensical idea of measuring performance quarter by quarter — or even year by year — many would hit the ceiling if an investment advisor failed to get rid of a stock that acted badly for more than a year or two."

And they would have missed a fantastic ride.

So, I use Phelps's method with my holdings. I usually go back only a decade. I use some different numbers, but I recommend keeping it simple. On page 48 is a table for one of my holdings, Copart. It's a good example because the business itself has been remarkably stable over time, even though the stock price has been

Year	Share Earnings	Dividends	Share Sales	Book Value	Return on Equity (%)
1970	$1.28	.63	$13.68	$7.67	16.6
1969	1.13	.57	12.73	6.94	16.2
1968	1.03	.50	11.85	6.77	15.6
1967	.96	.48	10.47	6.11	15.6
1966	1.02	.48	10.32	5.49	18.6
1965	.90	.43	9.01	4.89	18.3
1964	.76	.38	8.04	4.48	16.8
1963	.69	.35	7.01	4.29	16.0
1962	.64	.32	6.64	4.16	15.3
1961	.58	.28	5.69	3.56	16.2
1960	.52	.27	5.37	3.34	15.7
1959	.50	.27	5.12	3.03	16.5
1958	.49	.25	4.56	2.73	18.0
1957	.47	.23	4.24	2.49	18.8
1956	.37	.19	3.75	2.25	16.5
1955	.33	.17	3.66	1.93	17.1
1954	.33	.15	3.29	1.75	18.8
1953	.30	.14	2.88	1.58	18.9
1952	.24	.13	2.44	1.53	15.7
1951	.27	.18	2.05	1.42	19.0

all over the place. For the purposes of this example, I picked out just three basic financial figures: sales, earnings per share (EPS), and return on equity (ROE).

Looking only at those figures, would you want to be trading in and out of this stock? Sales and earnings per share have marched steadily upward over the years. Return on equity has been strong, though it has declined in recent years as the company built up cash. We will look at the importance of reinvesting profits in later chapters. For now, it is enough to say results fluctuate. A business,

COPART À LA PHELPS'S TABLE

Year	Sales ($B)	EPS	ROE (%)
2006	0.5	0.07	10.2
2007	0.6	0.10	15.5
2008	0.8	0.12	19.7
2009	0.7	0.11	15.4
2010	0.8	0.11	14.0
2011	0.9	0.16	30.0
2012	0.9	0.18	32.5
2013	1.0	0.18	23.7
2014	1.2	0.18	17.9
2015	1.1	0.23	22.8
2016	1.3	0.31	35.1
2017	1.4	0.43	35.9
2018	1.8	0.45	26.5
2019	2.0	0.64	33.3
2020	2.2	0.74	28.2
2021	2.7	0.99	26.6
2022	3.5	1.14	23.6
2023	3.9	1.29	20.7
2024	4.2	1.42	18.2
2025	4.6	1.59	18.5

like a professional athlete, is not at the top of its game every year. But you don't need it to be. You need the business to be good enough over a long period of time. The stock price will follow.

And it did. Copart's stock was up about 25x from 2006 to 2025. Of course, the ride to 25x was not as easy as the financials suggest. There were sharp drawdowns and periods of lagging the market averages, including a drawdown of nearly 30% as I write this. (See nearby chart.) There were also economic worries, bumbling central bankers, fiat currency, and other bad stuff during those 20 years. The stock was cut in half in the financial crisis in 2008-09 and nearly cut in half again during the pandemic of 2020.

Again, if you focused on the company results alone and thought like a business owner, you wouldn't have sold Copart.

So, I recommend creating "Phelps's Tables" for all your stocks. Keep these tables nearby and update them. Though a backward-looking exercise, it can help you through periods when the market drops significantly by giving you perspective.

COPART: 20 YEARS

25-bagger with numerous drawdowns

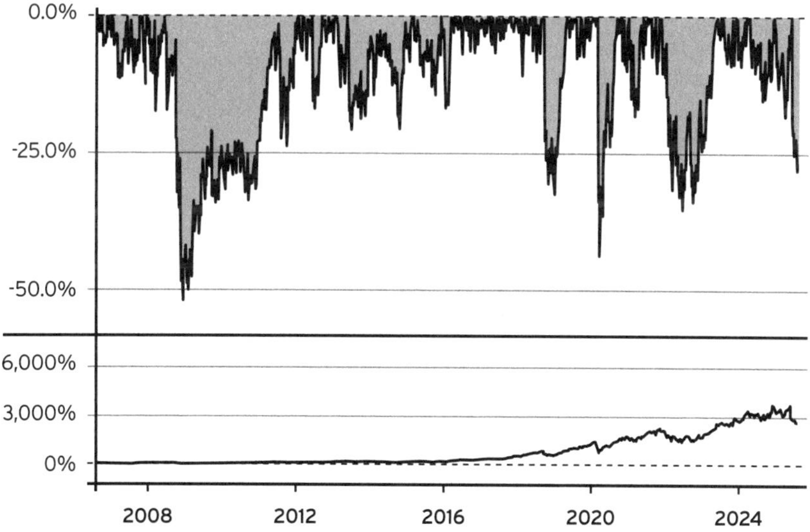

These tables may also reveal something else; they may expose all the poor businesses you own. "But each investor must judge for himself," Phelps writes, "primarily because he knows himself better than anyone else does."

The journey home to Ithaca is long and full of trials. If you want to enjoy those wonderful multi-baggers — if you want to have a shot at multiplying your money 100-fold, or more — then accept the challenge Thomas Phelps lays down:

> **"The secret of success in your quest for 100-to-one stocks is to focus on earnings power rather than prices. Can you do it?"**

If you don't get a 100-bagger, so what? The idea is to think big, to play for a big prize. Great putters try to hole every putt, even though they know they won't make them all. Investors need to think like great putters. If you follow these ideas, you could still be richly rewarded over time, even if you never get a 100-bagger. Those who never try are guaranteed never to succeed.

A Real Estate Mindset

Another strategy to keep from turning over your portfolio is more of a mindset change when buying a stock in the first place: Think of buying a stock as you would think of buying real estate.

For more on this perspective, I'd like to bring back Robert Kirby, who we met earlier. Every essay I come across by him seems wise and witty. One such essay comes from a collection by various contributors on the 50th anniversary of the great crash of 1929. Kirby's essay is titled "Lessons Learned and Never Learned." Kirby notes that most of those who experienced the 1929 crash were out of the business by 1979, and had been for 15 years or more.

And so the lessons of the crash go, too. Kirby complains, in his usual eloquent way, how investors of 1979 were trying hard to make it look like they were investing. They researched, consulted industry experts, talked to management, built models, etc., but mostly, they wound up chasing performance. They bought what was hot, then tried to justify it.

Kirby thought that if it were more challenging to sell what you bought, you'd think more carefully before buying. He used the example of real estate. You can't easily buy and sell real estate the way you can publicly listed stocks. Real estate transactions involve a lengthy and costly process by comparison.

So, when you buy real estate for an investment, you think more carefully about what you're doing. Professional real estate investors focus on the internal rate of return that asset is likely to generate if they had to retain their ownership for an indefinite period.

Extending that thinking to ownership of stocks sounds boring, and even irrelevant. Who cares about the internal rate of return when Nvidia doubles in six months? But over long periods of time, it does matter. (We'll get to what drives long-term returns in Chapter 5).

Therefore, Kirby said you should run a portfolio of common stocks like a real estate portfolio. You project future cash flows and expenses of the business and focus on the potential cash return it earns compared to what you paid to own it. This sounds sensible.

Of course, real estate gets crazy too, so his analogy loses some of its force today. It was getting nutty in Kirby's time, too, and he paused to note the irony, but he made his point. We should consider what return a business earns (or potentially earns) on its capital. Chuck Akre takes this approach as well and I think of his oft repeated favorite phrase, "The bottom line of all investing is rate of return."

Anchored by Conviction

For seven years (70%!) of Odysseus' journey home to Ithaca, he was a prisoner of the nymph Calypso. Despite her temptations, Odysseus held firm in his conviction to get home to wife Penelope. Investors need conviction as well, which reminds me of a lunch I had with Preston Athey, who used to manage the T. Rowe Price Small-Cap Value Fund. In his 20-plus years at the helm, his fund consistently earned 12% annually, easily surpassing all benchmarks. He stepped down in 2014 and is now retired. I count him among the best investors I know.

When I told him I had started a fund, his first question was, "What's your ideal turnover?"

"Well ... ideal?" I said. "Ideally, it'd be zero."

"That's the right answer," he said.

I first met Athey in 2012 after he gave a talk at a Baltimore CFA event. His talk was full of timeless wisdom. One of the things he talked about was buying stocks for keeps. When he ran his fund, his turnover was around 10%. That implies a holding period of ten years.

Not too many people can hold on to stocks like that. Then again, there aren't many investors of Athey's caliber At our first meeting, we discussed the coffee can portfolio idea. We're both fans of the idea, which as mentioned is a kind of crutch to help you hold on to your stocks longer.

While at T. Rowe, Athey studied Morningstar's mutual fund database. He examined all nine style boxes: value and growth, large cap and small cap, etc., and compared the top funds with the worst-ranked funds, and with the average funds.

In all nine cases, the higher-rated funds had lower turnover than the lower-rated funds. "In essentially every study we've done, this holds," Athey said. Put another way, funds that held onto their stocks did better than those that traded them.

Does this mean that if you trade less, you will do better?

No, there is no cause-and-effect relationship. Low turnover is a residual effect or a reflection of something else — conviction and patience.

If you know what you own and why you bought it, you're less likely to be shaken out when the stock drops. You only panic when you don't know what you own, and so you rely on the price and what other people are saying.

Athey's career shows incredible conviction. As mentioned, he had a turnover rate of just 10%. And half of that turnover, Athey said, came from takeovers in which he had no choice — the stock was taken away from him.

In short, take the time to know what you buy before you buy. And buy only those ideas for which you have a firm conviction. Ask yourself, "If the stock fell by 25% in a general market drawdown, are you a buyer?" If you can't answer yes, you don't have conviction in the name. Resist the urge to trade in and out of stocks. Aim to lengthen your holding periods.

Make Haste Slowly

Holding on to your stocks longer and aiming for higher returns might sound counterintuitive, even paradoxical. It's as if I'm telling you that in order to get where you want to go faster, you have to slow down. There's actually an old Latin phrase that captures this idea, *"Festina lente."*

I first read the term in *The Art of Worldly Wisdom: A Pocket Oracle,* a book written in 1647 by Baltasar Gracian, who was a witty Jesuit from Spain. His book of 300 aphorisms, with his commentary on them, has been translated into many languages and has earned the praise of philosophers ever since.

Some of the advice is straightforward, for example, "Never compete with someone who has nothing to lose." Some of it is familiar — "Mind your own business." And you will surely disagree with some, such as, "Don't keep company with those who will make you seem less gifted." His commentary on these maxims can be digressive and fragmentary. But all of it is entertaining and thoughtful.

Anyway, there is a passage where Gracian talks about the motto *Festina lente.* This Latin phrase is usually translated as "make haste slowly." One must be very patient and yet ready to act swiftly. And the fastest way to achieve your goals is sometimes by doing nothing.

The motto was a favorite of the Roman Emperor Augustus.

Engravers captured the idea with an emblem of a dolphin wrapped around an anchor, which they stamped on coins. Another emblem captured the same idea with a crab and a butterfly, again marrying this idea of fast and slow.

In investing, as we've seen, harnessing the powers of compounding requires you to sit still most of the time. This seems obvious on reflection, but it is hard because everything in our culture nudges us to do something.

Thus, giving in to those pressures, people often engage in counterproductive behavior. A quote from Akre Capital Management nails it:

> "Examples of such counterproductive behavior are well known to all of us: trying to sell before the next recession, trying to buy just before the next bull market, "repositioning" portfolios based on what is supposed to do better in the new paradigm, dumping stocks during a downturn, which deprives oneself of the means to eventually recover. People do these things because they are intuitive. After all, these actions appear rational in the face of heightened concern and uncertainty. **This is precisely why compounding over the long term is so challenging and rare: it demands counter-intuitive and seemingly irrational behavior."** [bold added]

It does seem incredibly counterintuitive to say, "No, you shouldn't try to sell before a recession," or, "No, you shouldn't 'reposition' your portfolio based on recent events." Don't these seem like logical things to do?

Not if you want to enjoy the fantastic effects of compounding capital over long periods of time. The main problem with these things is that they are too hard to do well enough. You have to commit to maintaining this kind of discipline over a lifetime of investing. The odds against you are considerable. Sure, you may be right sometimes. But you will most certainly sit out stretches of time during which you could have earned excellent returns because you're afraid of a recession. Odds are you won't get those "repositionings" right repeatedly either.

Consider the decisions you have to make during a single year, trying to call the twists and turns of the market. What a frazzled existence.

During bear markets, the temptation to do something is even greater. And it is during these times when it is most important to sit still. As Gracian wrote during the bear market of 1647:

> "Leave things alone. Especially when the sea – people, your friends, your acquaintances – is stirred up … It takes little to muddy a stream. You can't make it grow clear by trying to, only by leaving it alone. There is no better remedy for disorder than to leave it alone to correct itself."

I'm kidding about the bear market of 1647. But Gracian, at times, sounds like he is giving Buffett-esque investment advice:

> "Know how to wait… Never hurry and never give way to your emotions… Fortune gives large rewards to those who wait."

Festina lente. Make haste slowly.

On Initial Public Offerings

Let's end this part about dos and don'ts by discussing the birth of every public company — its first listing or initial public offering. I'm sure you've heard people ask, "Why would you look at a new IPO? Don't they do poorly? Aren't you almost guaranteed to get a bad price?" (This does not apply if you can get shares before they go public. It's a well known phenomena to get that first-day pop).

I know why people say this. A quick search online brings back lots of negative articles on the performance of IPOs. To wit, from *Kiplinger* in 2021:

> "Long-term IPO returns are nothing to brag about... IPOs that were bought at the first day's closing price and held for 48 months posted a median decline of 17.4%, according to research firm IPOX Schuster, citing data from 1985 through 2019. Nearly 57% of IPOs in that four-year holding period had negative returns. 'Most IPOs will underperform,' says firm founder Josef Schuster."

The "base rate" of investing in IPOs doesn't look too favorable. But be careful about drawing such broad conclusions, especially regarding investing, where the outliers tend to drive performance.

Arguably, the base rate for investing in equities is poor, not just IPOs. Bessembinder's famous study found that most stocks didn't beat the return on one-month treasury bills. The top-performing 2.4% of stocks accounted for all the stock market wealth creation from 1990 to mid-2020.

So, should we ditch equities altogether? Or should we see what kinds of stocks outperform?

If you were to put in place some simple guardrails, such as investing only in profitable companies, that would knock out most IPOs in most years. What would happen then?

And what if you stuck with reasonable valuations, high-quality insiders with proper incentives, in moaty businesses with good growth, and high returns on capital?

In other words, should you care if a stock is an IPO? I don't think so. Instead, run it through the same underwriting process as anything else. Ignoring a stock automatically because it has the "IPO" label stuck to it strikes me as arbitrary.

Many of these studies have short time horizons. What does performance look like after a decade?

I think some investors don't like to look at fresh IPOs because there is a general feeling of unease at buying something so obviously and recently "sold." All those investment bankers hawking the shares, the hype, the excitement — these things don't seem conducive to getting a great deal.

Except that every business you own in the public market is a business the original owner sold. The stock market is a market of second-hand goods. Every 100-bagger was once an IPO. Microsoft was once an IPO. So were Tractor Supply and Monster Beverage and Home Depot, and the rest of them.

Think about that. This original owner (or owners) presumably knew more about the business than anyone. And they sold it, or parts of it.

This tells us at least one thing — people who sell things don't know what the future will bring any more than people who buy things.

For example, Vincent Bollore, a well-regarded capital allocator, sold Universal Music Group. "Well," some investors think, "I'd be wary of buying from him. He's a smart guy!" Yes, he is. But he also sold Activision Blizzard in 2014. Specifically, he sold 41.5 million shares for about $20.5 each. In 2022, Microsoft bid $95 per share and eventually bought it out. With dividends, Bollore missed out on almost 5x in 8-9 years (20% CAGR).

I am sure some investors thought, "Gee, Bollore is selling. He's a smart guy. I'm going to follow him." Worse, Bollore took some of those proceeds and bought Telecom Italia. While Activision Blizzard was up almost 5x, Telecom Italia cut in half.

No one knows the future. Not even the original owners. Not even insiders. And we all make mistakes.

We're ready now to look at what kind of vessel we want to take on this journey. Our lady made a wise choice in Berkshire Hathaway. What do we want to look for in choosing our vessel? In the next section, we'll take a look at what makes a great business.

TOP TAKEAWAYS

1. *Resist the Siren songs and focus on what matters.*
2. *"Big picture" concerns are not that important in the long run.*
3. *Forecasts forget how people react and change their behavior: Chewing tobacco and horse manure did not destroy New York City.*
4. *Remember the horse story, and be humble about what seems like a setback or a victory today. The long haul will reveal many reversals.*
5. *Don't watch stock prices during the day. Don't watch financial coverage on TV or online, look at top-performing stocks you don't own, agonize over stocks you wish you bought, and focus on what* should *happen.*
6. *Ignore surveys or at least question who is being surveyed and what they know (or don't know).*
7. *Don't rely on the media. Remember the smoking priests and reduce your media intake.*
8. *Make tables of key financial stats of your stocks, by year, for several years. Scrutinize these performance numbers, not stock prices.*

9. *Own stocks like you would own real estate. Think carefully before you buy.*

10. *Conviction helps you stay the course. Ideally, it reduces your portfolio's stock turnover to zero.*

11. *Remember* festina lente *(make haste slowly). When it comes to investing, sometimes the fastest way to achieve your goal is to do nothing.*

12. *Don't automatically shun IPOs. Every 100-bagger was once an IPO. Evaluate IPOs as you would any other opportunity.*

CHAPTER 3

What a Great Business Looks Like

SO, LET'S START with the ideal. What is the best business to own?

Over the years, my appreciation for Buffett's succinct encapsulation of investing wisdom has grown. In the following single sentence, Buffett has captured the essence of what you should look to buy: "The best business to own is one that over an extended period can employ large amounts of incremental capital at very high rates of return."

I remember thinking, "Gosh, that does say everything." It's from Buffett's 1992 shareholder letter, where he goes on to make the point that growth only benefits investors if the business can invest at incremental returns that are attractive. For example, if every dollar reinvested in the business creates $2 of additional cash flow, you'd want that business to reinvest as many dollars as possible. By contrast, if a business needs to invest $50 to generate an additional dollar of free cash flow, you wouldn't want it to reinvest. Those returns matter and add up over time.

There is a table that I frequently use in presentations I give to my investors, which illustrates the value of what Buffett is saying. It shows a business that begins with $100 in capital and earns a 20% return on that investment. It reinvests all of its profits. After ten years, the capital in the business will grow to $619. (See the table on the following page.)

That's tremendous value creation and puts the valuation into perspective. Assuming you have a high conviction that this business can put up these kinds of numbers over a decade, you should not care too much about paying 20x earnings, 25x earnings, or 35x earnings, because the business is going to increase in size sixfold. You have a lot of room for error. (Even if the multiple you paid gets cut in half over the decade, you will still earn 3 times your initial investment, or nearly 12% annually).

Year	Capital ($)
0	100
1	120
2	144
3	173
4	207
5	249
6	299
7	358
8	430
9	516
10	619

And this is only for a period of 10 years. For 20 years, the increase would be 38x from year one. Just five years more, and the increase jumps to almost 100x over the whole 25-year period.

You can also see how paying a dividend would be an unwise decision in this case. If this company paid out half of its cash flow in dividends, then it will not compound its capital at anywhere near this rate. Yes, you will have the cash, net of taxes, but unless you can readily reinvest at rates better than this company, the rational decision is to have the company reinvest it.

So, again, the best businesses are those that can reinvest

substantial amounts of money at high rates of return for an extended period. (This is essentially what Berkshire did.) The worst businesses are those that have to, or will, do the opposite; meaning they consistently invest ever-greater amounts at low rates of return. As Buffett points out, the first type of business is tough to find.

That's the ballgame right there. Our goal is to find companies that can do what Buffett says. So now that we have an idea about what kind of vessel we want, we need a crew. How do we think about the people manning the vessel? We'll take a look in the next chapter.

TOP TAKEAWAYS

1. *The best businesses to own are those that can employ large amounts of capital at high rates of return.*
2. *A 20% return yields a 6x return over 10 years, 38x over 20 years and nearly 100x over 25 years.*
3. *Such returns put valuation in perspective.*
4. *Dividends slow the compounding of high return businesses.*

CHAPTER 4

Trustworthy Stewards

AS WE CONSIDER our crew, I suggest we keep one truism in mind — owners think differently from hired hands.

Sam Walton started Walmart in 1962. He was a dominant shareholder for years. Walton famously lived modestly. He drove his own pickup truck. He obsessed over operations, visiting stores personally. Every dollar he saved and every efficiency gained directly compounded his fortune. That's the kind of alignment we investors love to see. And it is hard to find.

Surely, it's not only ownership that led to such behaviors. Certainly, Sam Walton also possessed a high degree of personal character. Nonetheless, ownership is a contributing factor. If he was just paid a salary and a bonus, would he have been the same Sam Walton? I find that hard to believe. Sam was destined to be the captain on his own ship.

Besides, we can find many examples throughout business history where a lack of ownership contributed to a very different sort of behavior.

Dick Fuld owned something like 1% of Lehman Brothers in 2007 before it went bust. Leveraged at over 30x, there wasn't much consequence to him if things went sour. Most of his compensation was in options, and he cashed out over $500 million of these options in the seven years before.

It seems obvious that if you are the CEO of a company and have a sizable financial stake in the business ("skin in the game"), you are going to behave differently than if you had no stake at all.

The value of having skin in the game was a lesson I learned

early from Martin Sosnoff (the minimalist investor we met in the Introduction), who had an unforgettable way of writing about it. One of my favorite coinages of his was, "Entrepreneurial instinct equates with sizable equity ownership."

Humble on Wall Street

Sosnoff has more wisdom to offer. His book *Humble on Wall Street* is a candid tale of managing money in the 1960s and 1970s. My copy is about to fall apart. I've got it well marked and have read it several times. It's not that Sosnoff's investing style is like my own, as I've said before. He's a very different kind of investor. But I love his writing style — punchy, metaphoric, and colorful.

We agree on the importance of having someone at the top with skin in the game. And when I think of Sosnoff, this is always the lesson I think of, along with Sosnoff's Law. He once told me that in the 1980s, he owned about 15% of the New York Times. The market valued the stock at about $3 billion. In 2015, the price was about the same as it was 30 years ago. By contrast, Sosnoff said, look at what Rupert Murdoch did. He was also in the newspaper business. His company was worth about $3 billion at the time. By 2015, this had grown to approximately $80 billion.

"It just shows you that in the long run, you've got to have good management," Sosnoff told me. "And you've got to stay with them. Buffett has the right idea. Good management will always surprise you by being innovative or by doing a deal." As Sosnoff puts it in *Silent Investor, Silent Loser,* "If you have caretaker management, you get caretaker results."

With chapter titles such as "The Case Against Custodial Management" and "The Enduring Rape of Shareholders," Sosnoff makes his intense dislike of kept boards and consultants and other parasites clear:

"Would you rather own a company whose management

> owns the business and minds the store 24 hours a day, or would you rather invest in a New York City Bank or a Fortune 100 company with a board of directors of two dozen insiders and passive outsiders, none of whom will ever own more than a token percentage of the equity?"

He gives several colorful examples of what managers with skin in the game tend to do. One of them is the story of John Kluge. While the old network broadcasters slumbered in their sleepy businesses, Kluge out-hustled them on the way to building a billion-dollar fortune in Metromedia. In 1987, he was the richest man in America according to Forbes. Sosnoff says the vast difference in performance between the custodial managers of most of the Fortune 500 and Kluge "boiled down to guts, brains, and a single-minded determination to advance the price of the stock based on improving the fundamental[s]." because he had a lot of skin in the game.

In stark contrast to owner-operators like Kluge, Sosnoff criticizes the typical uninvested boards of most companies. For example, he gives us a fine example of what to avoid in International Paper. It had $5 billion in revenues and earnings power of just $100 million. Its twelve directors collectively owned 74,740 shares of the 50 million outstanding. No director owned as much as one-tenth of 1%. And why should they? As Sosnoff says, the return on equity has drifted downward for a decade, averaging less than 7% in the previous five years, and just 3% in 1985. This lethal combination of management's negligible equity stake and the poor returns to shareholders is a bright red flag to stay away.

And just to keep our fine lady from Nantucket in mind, Buffett was the largest shareholder of Berkshire Hathaway for many decades and as I write this in late 2025, he is still the largest shareholder.

Pay attention to that proxy. Pay attention to management's incentives. Pay attention to who owns the shares and what kind of incentives they have. A highly motivated and properly incentivized team can produce excellent results over time.

Somewhat related is the broader question of corporate culture. After all, the ship needs more than a great captain. It needs a great crew. And the same principles apply. We want owners, which is not always practical. But we want an ownership mentality or culture among the crew. There are ways to achieve this, which we will see in the next section.

How to Assess Corporate Culture

Investors talk about corporate culture, but what does that mean? What's a good corporate culture?

Culture is challenging to define and evaluate, but it encompasses areas such as how a business interacts with its employees, customers, and suppliers. It also covers how a business pays and incentivizes its employees (including its executives). Those are some things that come to mind when I think about culture. And some of these are easier to assess than others.

For example, let's consider employees. Sometimes, you get clues in the 10-K (the annual report in the US).

Brown & Brown, the insurance broker, has a whole section in their 10-K titled "Culture." In that section, for the year 2022, they share this:

> "Over 20% of our Company is owned by teammates, which we believe cultivates a unique ownership culture. We strive to provide multiple opportunities for teammates to share in the ownership of Brown & Brown and to help create personal wealth, including through our Employee Stock Purchase Program, 401(k) plan, and long-term equity grants. With more than 60% of our teammates owning stock in our Company, we operate with an ownership mindset that influences how we invest in our business and the work we do for our customers."

Well, that's what we want, isn't it? We want an ownership

culture. If you see something like this, it is probably an indication of a good culture. It's not the only thing, but it is something. Perhaps this contributes to Brown & Brown's industry-leading free cash flow conversion rate and its long-term market-beating performance.

We can also consider how long employees tend to stay. If a company treats its staff right, then you'd expect a lower turnover than average. Sometimes, companies comment on employee turnover in their 10-K.

Consider Old Dominion Freight Lines, a trucking company. To be more specific, they are one of the largest less-than-truckload carriers in the United States. Less-than-truckload (LTL) is, as the name suggests, carrying loads that do not take up a full truck.

Reading Old Dominion's 10-K, I found this:

> "The 10-year average turnover rate for our driver graduates is approximately 6.9%, which is below our 10-year average turnover rate for our Company-wide drivers of approximately 9.8%."

Old Dominion invests in its employees by providing a training program. Drivers who complete that program tend to stay with the company longer than others. That 9.8% turnover rate is low for trucking anyway, which is another indication of a good work culture.

In addition to employees, how businesses interact with their customers can provide valuable insights. This is where expert networks, such as In Practise, and others, can help. Sometimes you get gems, like this one from an Old Dominion customer, published by Tegus:

> "Old Dominion really has a customer service, customer satisfaction model throughout their company. And I include the drivers in that, I include the dispatches in that all the way up to the CEO of the company. They really care about things.
>
> When I have a problem with Old Dominion, I can pick

> up the phone and I can immediately get a manager on the phone at almost any place in the country, and they will do everything they possibly can to solve my problem right then. So if I call [the competitor] Saia, I'm lucky if I get anybody, but one of the regional dispatchers to talk to me. And usually, their answer is there's nothing I can do about it."

Now, this is just one person's opinion. But if you get a string of similar comments from different people, you may be on to something.

In Practise is another expert network focused particularly on quality companies and is the one I rely on. There are many examples I could pull from transcripts that show good culture at work. Just one more example from a transcript covering Constellation Software, a much admired firm and a big winner since its IPO in 2006:

> "[Constellation] is a hard place to work, but awesome if you want to learn and grow and have long-term value creation. They also take risks on and invest in people, which has documented... Performance management and people development is a huge part of it. Every time I saw [CEO] Mark Miller in the hallway he asked me, what are you doing to grow your people? I hear John Doe is really awesome; how are you going to make him a portfolio leader?"

We want this. We want to see a company invest in its people. We want a performance-based culture, which Constellation has in spades.

We can also think of Berkshire. It was largely decentralized. The subsidiary companies had a high degree of autonomy. As Buffett put it in his owner's manual, "we delegate almost to the point of abdication." There were no budgets, no strategic plans, none of the corporate bureaucracy that slowed other similar large organizations. Buffett constantly praised his managers and they tended to stick with Berkshire and deliver good results over a long period of time. People seemed to like working there. Just read Buffett's letters and you have plenty of examples of good corporate culture at work.

You'll also find that good cultures tend to accompany winning firms, which is why we want to pay attention to culture as a potential leading indicator of continued future performance for the business. Old Dominion has been taking market share at about one-percentage point per year and has industry-leading metrics in all the essential categories: on-time delivery, claims, etc. It also has industry-leading return on invested capital (ROIC) metrics, by a wide margin.

So while culture is difficult to define and assess as an outsider, it seems to be an aspect of a winning business. Some would even call it a competitive advantage.

As you can probably gather by now, when you start with the idea of owning a business for a decade or more, your attention shifts away from what the media and other investors think is essential — a focus on the valuation multiple, for example — to a different set of concerns, the ability to reinvest and earn high returns for many years to come, and the culture of the business.

This shift in perspective is profound. It colors everything you do in investing, from quarterly earnings reports to market turmoil. It certainly impacts how you evaluate companies.

TOP TAKEAWAYS

1. *Owners think differently than hired hands; we want to invest with owners.*

2. *"Entrepreneurial instinct equates with sizable equity ownership." — Martin Sosnoff*

3. *Don't forget the crew. Assess corporate culture by evaluating how the business treats and incentivizes employees.*

CHAPTER 5

What Drives Investment Results

NOW, WE ARE READY to examine the details of what drives investment returns. What are the sources of the great returns enjoyed by the lady from Nantucket with her Berkshire stock, or Sam Walton from his Walmart shares?

We've looked at a few contributing factors already. We've considered the critical importance of a business reinvesting profits at high rates of return, of having insiders with skin in the game and a good corporate culture. But *time* is the fundamental point that joins many of these attributes together. The quality of a business and its crew reveals itself over a longer horizon. They don't matter much in the short term.

So, before we can answer what drives investment returns, we need to ask ourselves, *what's my time horizon?* Because different factors come into play depending on your perspective.

For example, you might hear someone say that "X stock is expensive" because it trades at a "high" multiple of earnings or cash flow. I usually respond that it depends on your time horizon. If you're a long-term investor, the kind we discuss in this book, you will have a different view than someone looking for a good gain but otherwise doesn't intend to hold the stock for years.

To set the stage, let me share one of my favorite charts on the following page.

I plan to own companies for at least ten years, which happens to be the time it took for Odysseus to get home, and ideally much

Source: Connor Leonard, Value Investing Club at Google, February 2019

longer. That's my mindset going in. So, I spend most of my time on the right side of this graphic: understanding the people and culture, figuring out incentives, the reinvestment opportunities, and the returns the company is likely to make on them.

I spend almost no time thinking about things like sentiment change or building a thesis around a change in multiples. Over a decade of ownership, those things don't matter much. Yes, there can be dramatic changes in multiples. You may be especially fortunate to own a stock that goes from a 10x multiple to 30x. So, let's say free cash flow is $1, and you paid $10 for the stock. The multiple is 10x. In ten years, the free cash flow reaches $4, and the stock trades for a multiple of 30 times free cash flow. Now the stock price is $120, or 12 times your initial purchase price, even though free cash flow "only" increased four times. Multiple expansion helps, but it's rare and difficult to accurately predict.

Conversely, going from 30x to 10x is painful. So, again, assume $1 in free cash flow. You paid $30 for the stock. Ten years later, the free cash flow is $4, but the stock trades for 10 times that, or $40. You've made a 33% return on your ten-year investment. Not good.

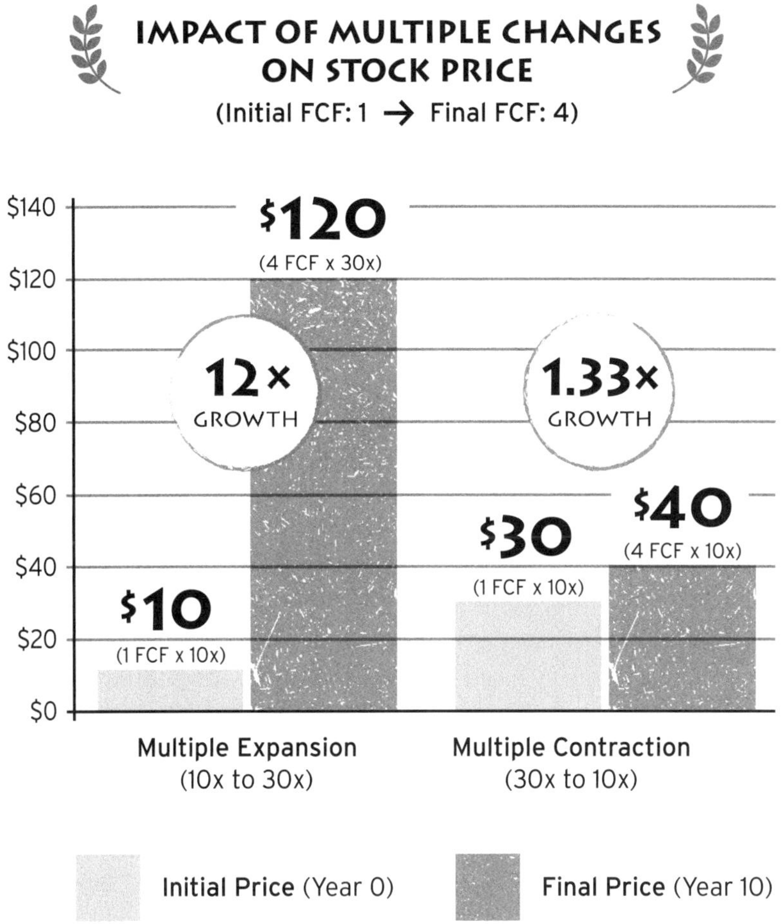

The price you pay is important. Please don't take away from this book that valuation doesn't matter. But the items on the right side of the time horizon chart are more important. If I don't have those, I'm not interested, even if the stock "looks cheap" on a multiple of free cash flow (or whatever your favorite ratio). The importance of the price you paid bleeds out over time if you own a high quality company compounding its capital at a high rate.

If you're right about the quality, you'll do okay unless you overpay significantly. If a business increases free cash flow by 20x, you're not going to mind much that you paid a 30% premium over what peers traded at when you purchased it. Even if you "overpay" by a lot more than that, you can still do well if you size it right, give yourself room to buy more later, and, most importantly, stick with it. (We'll get more into portfolio building later in the book.)

But you've got to be right about the business. You won't be able to complete the investor's odyssey in a leaky ship that sinks midway through, no matter how cheaply you bought it. And that's why the bulk of my focus and research is on the right side of that chart.

The Alchemy of Stock Market Performance

In the *Odyssey,* King Aelous entrusted Odysseus with a bag. The bag contained all the strong winds, but not the gentle west wind, which would carry him home. That is, as long as Odysseus did not open the bag and release the storm winds. Well, Odysseus took a nap and his crew greedily opened the bag expecting treasures. Instead, they released the storm winds, which blew the ship way off course.

The storm winds are the things many investors tend to focus on. Three popular favorites are changes in the valuation multiple, sentiment shifts, and industry cycles. These things are all more on the left hand part of the Time Horizon chart, and relatively unpredictable. But greedy for quick treasures, investors often open the bag and get blown off course from their journey towards wealth creation.

The gentle west wind is return on capital. A persistently high return on capital drives stock prices ever up — not just for a few months or a year, but over a decade or more. However, it seems to be widely under-appreciated. Financial journalists appear entirely unaware of it. And it leads to counterintuitive conclusions for most people, especially non-investors. Let's take a look at these mysteries.

The 7th edition of *Valuation,* by Tim Koller, Marc Goedhart, and David Wessels (KG&W), deals with this central question. (I took the title of this section from the heading of Chapter 5.) The only previous edition I had read was the second, when it came out in 1994. The Dow was only about 3,700 back then. And Jeff Bezos had just left DE Shaw to start Amazon in his garage. It was a different world. And that book was an entirely different book.

Anyway, I like the 7th edition's anecdotes, which pepper its pages and demonstrate the importance of what we've been discussing.

For example, consider the case of Costco versus Brown-Forman. Costco is the fourth-largest retailer in the US. Sales topped $126 billion in 2017. Brown-Forman produces Jack Daniel's and other boozy beverages. Sales were $4 billion in the same year.

From 1996 to 2017, Costco's profits increased at an annual rate of 11%, making it one of the fastest-growing companies in the US during that period. In contrast, Brown-Forman's profits grew at a rate of 7%. This significant difference meant that by the end of 2017, Costco's profits were nine times larger than they had been in 1996, while Brown-Forman's profits were only four times as large.

And yet, shareholders in both companies earned returns of about 15% annually. How so? First, we have to consider return on invested capital, or ROIC. It measures the profits a company generates against the amount of capital it took to generate those profits. (See Appendix, "Return on Invested Capital Calculation" for details).

Obviously, a higher ROIC is preferable. If you can generate $100 in profits with only $500 in invested capital, that's better than generating $100 in profits with $1,000 in capital. So, in our example, we have a business with a 20% ROIC (assuming $100 in profits and $500 in invested capital). But what if we reinvest those profits back into the business and that additional investment brings $25 in additional profits? Then our return on incremental invested capital (ROIIC) would be 25%. This is a great situation to find if the company can sustainably reinvest profits at a higher return (ROIIC) than its trailing return (ROIC), because it's a signal that ROIC will rise over time, which will favorably impact the valuation and future wealth creation over time. (In this book, henceforth, I'll just refer to ROIC for simplicity's sake, but you should know about ROIIC and keep an eye on it.)

Getting back to Costco vs Brown-Forman, the authors of *Valuation* write:

> "The reason Brown-Forman could create the same value as Costco, despite much slower growth, was that Brown-Forman earned a 29% ROIC (excluding the impact of acquisitions), while Costco's ROIC was 13%." (In other words, BF created more profits with much less capital relative to Costco.)

Mini-case studies like this are bite-sized chocolates for us investors. This particular example illustrates the fundamental framework of their book, summed up by the authors:

> "The amount of value a company creates is governed ultimately by its ROIC, revenue growth, and ability to sustain both over time."

Sound familiar? It's what Warren Buffett says. It's also the formula for 100-baggers. ROIC and growth concepts are mathematically linked, and the *Valuation* authors break them down for you in great detail. But suffice it to say that in the Costco-BF example, high ROIC was the equalizer for BF against Costco's superior growth.

Another dramatic example is Rockwell Automation. From 1995 to 2018, Rockwell's revenues fell from $13 billion to $7 billion as it divested its aviation and power systems businesses. Despite this massive shrinkage, shareholders enjoyed returns of 19% annually.

How so? You probably guessed it. The authors inform us that ROIC increased from 12% to "about 35% (including goodwill)."

But investing is not this simple. If it were, we could all just screen for high ROICs, buy those stocks, and go to sleep. In the real world, it is not so easy to identify companies that will maintain or raise their ROIC over 10-15 years. Not to mention that stock price volatility, bad news, quirks of human psychology, and other factors make it hard to hold on to anything.

My choice of 10-15 years is deliberate. The authors maintain that share prices align with a company's performance "over long periods, at a minimum, 10 to 15 years," which is kind of distressing. It means you might have to wait a very long time while your unthinking friends clean up on the latest meme stock.

Beyond the anecdotes (and logic), there is considerable empirical evidence supporting the ROIC framework, which the authors cover. We won't go through it here, but I want you to know such support exists. In short, keep the bag of winds closed and let the gentle west wind (ROIC) take you home.

Focus on "Economic Profit"

So, should a firm try to maximize its ROIC? If it can invest more capital at a lower return on capital but still earn a good return, then yes.

Here's an extreme example. Say you invested $10,000 and earned 100% returns. Now, let's say you have the opportunity to invest an additional $10,000, but you will earn a 50% return on this second tranche. Do you pass on the opportunity because it will lower your overall return on capital?

No, because you realize that a 50% return is attractive. And you'd rather put another $10,000 to work at 50% than sit on it or invest it in the alternatives.

Of course, it's not so obvious in the real world, and our returns are never certain. But the logic is clear. You prefer to invest as long as the returns are good.

Coming back to the 7th edition of *Valuation,* authors KG&W present a case study involving two entrepreneurs, Lily and Nate, who run a chain of clothing stores, and face a similar decision. They can close underperforming stores to raise their return on capital. Should they do it?

KG&W says Lily and Nate should focus on "economic profit,"

which they define as the difference, or spread, between your return on capital and your cost of capital multiplied by the amount of capital invested. You can think of the cost of capital as your opportunity cost. If you didn't invest it, this is what you'd get. (That's not exactly right, but it's okay for our purposes here.) So when I say a return is "good", I mean that the return is above your opportunity cost, or cost of capital.

Lily and Nate have a business with an 18% ROIC. They can improve it to 19% by cutting underperforming stores and freeing up $2,500 in capital. But should they do it? KG&W says no, because it will lower their economic profit.

Here's the table they use to make the point:

	ROIC (%)	Cost of Capital (%)	Spread (%)	Invested Capital	Economic Profit
Entire company	18	10%	8%	$12,000	$960
Without low performing stores	19	10%	9%	9,500	855

Another way to think about it is that if you had $2,500 back in capital, you could only reinvest it at 10%, i.e. your cost of capital. Obviously, you'd prefer 18%.

KG&W's advice to Lily and Nate is counterintuitive to many people. Most people would instead cheer for a company that closes underperforming stores, frees up capital, and increases its ROIC. But it may just be the call of the Sirens and not the right one. At least not if you have set sail for a longer journey and want to maximize the force of compounding.

This decision-making process concerning when and where to invest profits, then, is an important driver of our returns. We'll take a look at capital allocation in the next chapter.

TOP TAKEAWAYS

1. *What will drive your investment return depends on your time horizon.*

2. *Investors sailing home to their kingdom should embrace the gentle west wind, return on capital (ROIC).*

3. *A persistently high ROIC drives stock prices ever up, not just for a few months or a year, but over a decade or more.*

4. *Avoid storm winds like changes in the valuation multiple, sentiment shifts, and industry cycles. These may blow you off course.*

5. *Valuation matters, but the price you paid bleeds out over time if you own a high quality company.*

6. *Focus on the economic profit. Lily and Nate (or you) are better off with 18% return on the total investment than with 19% on one part and 10% on the rest.*

CHAPTER 6

What the Best Do With Their Profits

BY NOW, I HOPE YOU SEE what I think is the most reliable recipe for creating investment results (perhaps 100 times your money). The recipe uses just two ingredients, like a kind of financial martini: high returns on capital plus the ability to reinvest again and again at those high rates. Stir. Add olives, if desired. (Valuation matters, too, but these two are essential.)

Be mindful of potential leaks, such as companies issuing shares. Another leak is dividends.

What if a company can reinvest at lower rates of return than it currently does? Yes, that could make sense, as we learned in the example with Lily and Nate in the previous chapter. Should a company follow such a path, even if it means they must cut the dividend?

Cutting Dividends to Create Value

For most people, cultural hurdles and biases complicate making proper capital allocation decisions. For one thing, many are wed to their dividends (I call this "dividend disease."), and lowering returns doesn't sound good.

This is partly why Mark Leonard's 2021 shareholder letter is such a remarkable document.

Leonard is the founder and president of Constellation Software, Inc., which I used earlier as an example of a company with a performance-based culture. Constellation has been a compounding machine for years, earning attractive returns on capital. Leonard and his team are widely regarded as among the best capital allocators around. Incidentally, in September, 2025, Leonard stepped down as CEO due to a health issue.

In his 2021 letter, succinct and powerful at only two pages, Leonard made two important announcements that most companies would struggle to make.

He began with Constellation's historical commitment to achieving a high return on capital. Such a high bar invariably meant they would let some good deals pass by. And so, unable to find enough deals to meet this high bar, they could pile up cash. They paid that cash out to shareholders as dividends.

Was that the right way to do it? At least one director made a different case, as Leonard says in his letter:

> "One of our directors has been calling me irresponsible for years. His thesis goes like this: [Constellation] can invest capital more effectively than the vast majority of [Constellation's] shareholders, hence we should stop paying dividends and invest all of the cash that we produce, even if it means lowering our hurdle rates."

Leonard finally agrees with that director. Henceforth, Constellation looked to invest more capital by lowering its previous high hurdle rate *in some cases.* (Leonard also said Constellation would stop paying special dividends and while he maintained the quarterly dividend "for now," he told investors, "if we are successful in finding better uses for our [free cash flow], the quarterly dividend will also be sacrificed.") Consequently, Leonard warned, Constellation's return on investors' capital would decrease.

I wonder how many CEOs could say such a thing. It doesn't sound good, but it's excellent news. Since Constellation was earning such high returns on capital, they could stand a slight degradation to put more capital to work.

You don't want to own Constellation's stock if you can't trust this team to make the right call on future deals. Given their track record of allocating capital over many years, I was in favor of their decision to reinvest more capital.

And that means I also loved the idea of cutting the dividend.

There is a widespread cultural bias against doing this. I love many of the Swedish serial acquirers, for example. But one thing I dislike is the automatic promise to pay a certain percentage of their profits as dividends. Here are firms with high returns on capital that seem to have plenty of opportunities to reinvest, yet they're automatically giving one-third to one-half of their cash profits back to shareholders instead of reinvesting it. I don't know what the cost of capital is for these shareholders. But I am fairly certain it's well below what the serial acquirers earn when they reinvest it.

It's not just Sweden, but all of Europe. When I wrote *100 Baggers,* some readers protested the section where I essentially advised people not to look for dividends. Thomas Phelps, the author of the first book on 100-baggers, called *100 to 1 In The Stock Market,* also saw dividends as costly. He wrote, "Dividends are an expensive luxury" because they slow down the potential rate of compounding capital.

Another way to view this is to recall the table I showed you earlier, which illustrates the power of Buffett's observation about the best businesses to buy. Let's add another column, but this time, the business is paying out half of its profits every year. (See the chart on the following page.)

As you can see, in year 10, capital has slightly more than doubled, which is a far cry from the sixfold increase we saw in the compounding table in Chapter 3, where the company reinvested all of its profits. Yes, you have also accumulated $159 in pre-tax dividends over the ten years (which you could reinvest or spend, however you choose). But even so, you can see that the value created is quite a bit less than if the company had reinvested everything.

Ideally, as a long-term investor focused on finding big winners, you want a firm that reinvests as much of its profits as possible at

Year	Capital ($)	Return	Profit	Dividend	Reinvest	Sum of Dividends
1	100	0.2	20	10	10	10
2	110	0.2	22	11	11	21
3	121	0.2	24	12	12	33
4	133	0.2	27	13	13	46
5	146	0.2	29	15	15	61
6	161	0.2	32	16	16	77
7	177	0.2	35	18	18	95
8	195	0.2	39	19	19	114
9	214	0.2	43	21	21	136
10	236	0.2	47	24	24	159

high rates of return. Any payout to you is a leak in that compounding cycle. At some point, dividends are wise when attractive reinvesting opportunities have been exhausted. But for a great business and a skilled capital allocator, that can be a long time in the future. Our lady from Nantucket invested in Berkshire Hathaway, after all. And Berkshire, more than 60 years since Buffett took control, has yet to pay a dividend.

Again, this only applies to those rare and exceptional businesses that can mix that classic financial martini. Many mediocre businesses with marginal returns and limited reinvestment opportunities should consider paying dividends. But I'm not interested in those. I'm interested in businesses like Constellation Software.

Sweden & Global Outperformers

We can see the power of reinvestment by looking at a group of Swedish companies built for reinvestment. First, let's set the stage.

The study, "Global Outperformers," by Dede Eyesan of Jenga Investment Partners, highlights stocks that returned 1,000% between 2012 and 2022.

One notable surprise is how favorably Sweden appears in this study.

Sweden produced 20 companies with a return of more than 1,000%, accounting for approximately 4.5% of the total population of outperformers, despite representing only 1.5% of the global capitalization (as defined in the study).

China had 34 outperformers to Sweden's 20, but China's market was 12 times the size of Sweden's. Keep in mind that Sweden has a population of just 10 million.

In terms of total outperformers, Sweden was 5th, beaten only by giants: the US, India, China, and Japan. So, it's quite a remarkable showing by the Swedes.

Before we jump to the conclusions, there are several notable limitations to consider. The biggest one is that where a company is listed does not tell you where its most significant markets are.

As Eyesan notes, the US is the largest source of revenue and profits for many outperformers in Asia and Europe. Among the Swedes, companies such as CellaVision, Invisio, and Biotage derived more than one-third of their revenue from the US. If you adjusted this list by geographic source of revenues, you'd get a different look.

Even so, why does Sweden produce so many winners?

Eyesan has a few thoughts. He cites innovation as one factor:

- "Sweden is the second most innovative country in the world according to the Global Innovation Index.
- "Sweden has the highest R&D expenditure as a % of GDP in Europe
- "Sweden has the ninth-best education system in the world."

I am somewhat skeptical about how much these things matter or whether it is even possible to measure them. He also cites a focus on global growth among the Swedes. "It is common for Swedish startups to benchmark against global peers even in their early days," writes Eyesan. He also points to government initiatives that encourage exports and international trade.

I also have some ideas, though they are anecdotal and not necessarily any better than Eyesan's guesses. For one thing, there seems to be more attention paid to capital allocation (despite the widespread "dividend disease") than I often find elsewhere. Many companies discuss, and even report, a metric such as "return on capital employed."

The Swedes also have a high level of trust and a legal framework that facilitates relatively easy and efficient business combinations and transactions. Thus, it is a suitable environment for business.

As 2026 begins, I have three Swedish companies in my portfolio. My natural inclination to find winners led me to Sweden, rather than a top-down view of the country.

In the end, however, numerous Swedish companies have shown the heavenly ability to generate strong returns on capital and reinvest most of their cash flows at attractive rates of return. How do they do it?

The Conventional Wisdom is Wrong on Acquisitions

Many successful Swedish companies reinvest by acquiring other companies, which might turn off some investors. After all, don't most acquisitions destroy value? I held this view for a long time myself. I unlearned it when I started studying companies that had achieved great success by acquiring other companies, numerous companies over a prolonged period. Constellation Software is Exhibit A here. (The company has done over 1,000 acquisitions since its founding in 1995). However, there are many others, including those Swedes.

There is a book that should forever change your opinion on mergers and acquisitions (M&A): *Deals from Hell: M&A Lessons that Rise Above the Ashes,* by Robert Bruner. If nothing else, the introduction and the first few chapters do the trick. Bruner shows that failures in M&A account for a small percentage of the total volume of M&A activity. He further demonstrates that M&A yields returns comparable to those of other corporate investment forms.

Conventional wisdom suggests that M&A is often a losing proposition, but the empirical evidence supporting this view is scant. Here is Bruner:

> "[A]n objective reading of more than 130 studies supports the conclusion that M&A *does* pay. These studies show that the shareholders of the selling firms earn large returns from M&A, that the shareholders of the buyers and sellers combined earn significant positive returns, and that the shareholders of buyers generally earn about the required rate of return on investment."

Bruner points out that the big failures get all the press. So, it tends to skew our view of what's happening. The track record of successful serial acquirers shows that the rewards for mastering M&A can be immense.

Notes from Stockholm

What makes a serial acquirer? As the name suggests, a large portion of the company's growth stems from acquiring smaller private companies that fit a specific template. Serial acquirers are typically decentralized, with the acquired companies enjoying quite a bit of autonomy. The free cash flow of these daughter companies is funneled to the mothership, where it is deployed in new acquisitions, dividends, or other uses. Typically, serial acquirers look to hold companies forever.

That's a fundamental outline. I have to say I'm not that fond of the label "serial acquirer" because it underplays what the better companies do, which gets me to my second observation.

Building a successful serial acquirer is not easy. It's not just buying many companies and trying to play a financial arbitrage game. Things can go wrong. A case study on this would be another Swedish company, Storskogen, a previously aggressive buyer of companies. (See the chart on the following page.)

BIG 4 VS. MSCI WORLD INDEX

Total Shareholder Return (TSR) including
Price Appreciation, Divident Reinvestment
and Corporate Actions (Splits)

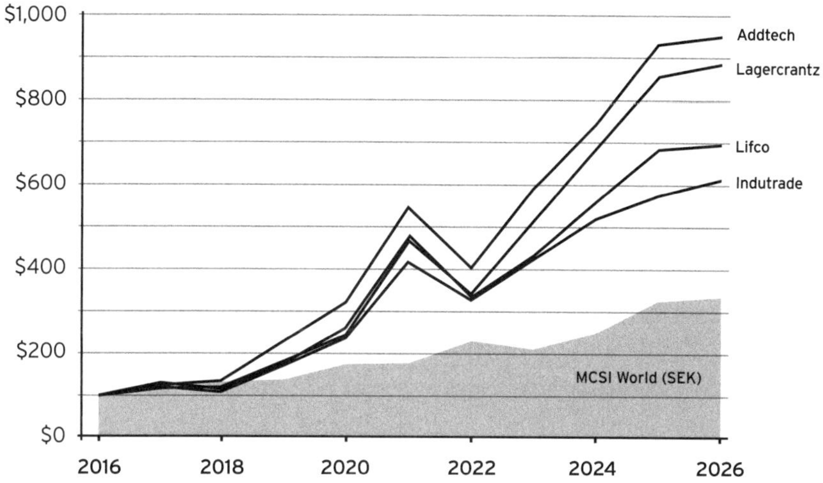

STORSKOGEN: 5 YEARS

10/6/2021 - 1/2/2026

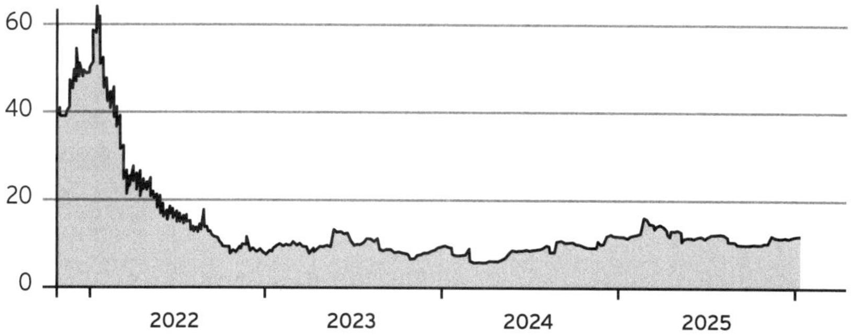

In short, Storskogen overpaid for companies of subpar quality. The intense acquisition spree was funded with cheap debt, which quickly got expensive when interest rates normalized. The group's earnings also declined, creating a toxic cocktail forcing the company to sell off businesses. What worked in a spreadsheet did not work out in reality.

In my studies of these structures, I found that the best are those that build companies. They are looking to buy something particular, an exceptional fit. Yes, there is a financial profile, whether based on return on capital employed, margins, sales growth, or whatever. However, there are also intangible qualities associated with culture, competitive position, complexity, and many other considerations. The best ones have built up a process over many years. They are focused on returns on capital.

Owning a serial acquirer is like owning a fund that buys private companies and aims to hold them indefinitely. (Not so different from our lady from Nantucket's Berkshire Hathaway). A publicly traded coffee can portfolio of sorts. It all comes down to a bet on capital allocation, a bet on the people and the process.

You learn some things during a visit that you might not pick up otherwise. Arriving at Lifco HQ, I was greeted by Per Waldemarson, the CEO, who was the only person there. The office was in a nice building, but was relatively modest and small. Most people are out in the field, and the headquarters is small for a company worth $16 billion.

You don't want to give too much weight to such things, but I can tell you not all companies give off the same vibes. I won't name names, but lavish office space is a warning that perhaps the focus is not where it should be.

Another thing I like about investing in serial acquirers is that you get some built-in diversification. You're getting a collection of different businesses. Slowdowns in one area may be offset by strength in another. As a group, I'd expect their financial results to be resilient.

Might there be better opportunities for serial acquirers when times are bad? Maybe. However, the concern is that good companies won't sell. They'll hold out because they know what they could've sold out for before and won't accept less.

While Sweden is dense with serial acquirers, there are others in the world. Let's learn from a long-time champion based in the UK.

Halma: How They Did It

Sometimes, a company's success starts very early in its history. It is either set on a good foundation, or it isn't. I suspect that many investors waste their energy on companies whose foundations were shaky initially and were thus doomed from the start.

Below is another delicious mini-case study about a company, another serial acquirer, whose founders laid a proper foundation and created enormous value.

That company is Halma, based in Amersham, England. It has been a public company since 1972, when the firm was founded (although it has roots dating back to earlier times). If I were to write a sequel to *100 Baggers* covering the UK market, I'd include Halma. Here's a look at the latest ten-year period in the chart on the following page.

Halma is a holding company with around 50 operating companies and generated sales of over £2.2 billion in 2024/2025 (fiscal year ended March 31). I will pass lightly over what these companies do, as I want to get to the broader DNA of why they've been so successful.

Halma's companies are involved in making the world safer, healthier, and cleaner. All their businesses focus on these broad areas. This includes various niches, such as fire detection, water analysis, food safety, and more. The economics are perhaps what binds them, per an August, 2004, *Financial Times* story:

> "A typical Halma business sells complex products, costing from £15 to £1,000, to an industrial customer in a niche market that is worth a few tens of millions of pounds annually. In products representing 30 percent of Halma's sales, Mr O'Shea [then CEO] says the company is the

HALMA: 10 YEARS

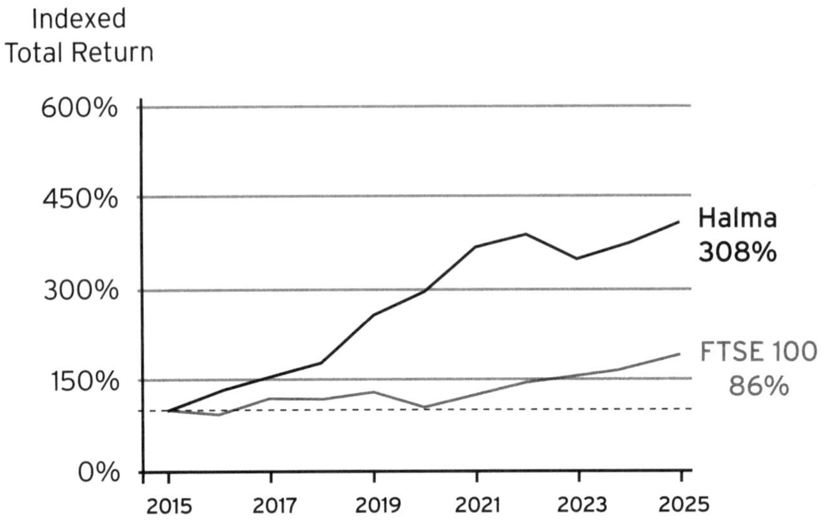

biggest in the world. In most of the other areas, it is one of just a few competitors."

When I talked to the company in 2020, they maintained that this was "broadly still true." Halma likes niche markets with global reach that address broader areas of safety, health, and the environment, where demographics and a rising tide of regulation drive growth.

So that's Halma. As I say, I'm passing lightly over the "what" aspect to get to the "how" part.

How They Did It

The "secret sauce," as it were, simmered early. On the company's website is a speech by David Barber, who co-founded Halma with Mike Arthur. Barber served as the CEO for over twenty years and as Chairman until his retirement in 2003. In his 1997 speech, "Delivering Shareholder Value," Barber reflected on what made

Halma's performance so great. At the time of the speech, Halma had delivered a 22.5% annualized increase in earnings per share for the prior 20 years.

Here are a few highlights from the speech:

Keep control over your shares outstanding

Halma targets a growth mix of 6-7% organically and 6-7% through acquisitions. Over time, they acquire a significant number of companies. They could have financed these in different ways, but early on, Barber and his team decided that since their main goal was to increase earnings per share, it would be better not to issue any shares (and make the job that much harder). This logic ran counter to the conventional view, which was to issue highly valued shares to fuel further growth.

However, as Barber points out, if a company is earning a 40% return on its capital and growing, you wouldn't sell it. That is a tradition that remains. Halma finances its acquisitions with internally generated cash flow. And its share count has barely moved over the last 20 years.

Compounding capital at high rates for an extended period is challenging enough. You don't want to make it harder by investing in companies that regularly issue shares. Share issuance is, as dividends, like a leak in a boat; it's something you have to overcome. Even small amounts of dilution, say 2% per year, add up over time. Dilution sneaks up on you.

The table on the following page shows you what growth in market cap is required for the stock price to stay constant over five years, at different rates of annual dilution.

As you can see, even 2% dilution requires an additional approximate 10% growth in market cap for the share price to stay even. Some companies manage to compile excellent track records despite steady dilution. Some boats manage to get from point A to point B, even though they leak. That's not a case for buying leaky boats. Dilution makes compounding more difficult, but not impossible. I tend to avoid serial issuers.

5 Year Market Cap Growth Required to Offset Dilution	
1% Dilution	5.1%
2% Dilution	10.4%
3% Dilution	15.9%
5% Dilution	27.6%
10% Dilution	61.1%

The recipe for successful acquisitions

Barber notes that "a large body of academic opinion" argues that most acquisitions fail to add value. We addressed this earlier. And Barber adds nuances to the kinds of acquisitions companies make. He warns that the word "acquisition" covers a wide range of activities, which are, in fact, very different from each other.

The first distinction he makes is between "acquisitions which are funded by internally generated surplus cash and those which are funded by share issues." He makes the following controversial claim:

> "Because we have funded acquisitions this way, the vast proportion of the wealth created within Halma has in fact come from organic growth. Ignoring scrip issues, our total shares in issue over the 24 years from 1973 to 1997 increased by only 46%. Over that same period, our pre-tax profit increased by 22,000%. So the first distinction I would draw is that growth by internally funded cash is more akin to organic growth than it is to growth by acquisition."

That's a good way to think about it and an easy filter to apply to any company you're considering. Do they acquire other companies primarily using internally generated cash, or do they borrow the money and/or issue shares?

Some very successful acquirers do it the way Halma does: Heico, Constellation Software, and Brown & Brown. They also keep control over their share count. In Constellation's case, it's unchanged since 2006.

Barber's other ingredient for success here is that the acquirer should stick to businesses it already knows. If you buy a business similar to something you already own, you're in a better position to know whether you got a good deal and how to manage it successfully. Barber found that this was the case for 70% of thc individual businesses Halma bought over the prior 15 years.

They did move into other businesses, but they moved cautiously. Ideally, they would buy small to reduce the impact if things went wrong.

Again, an easy filter — is the acquirer buying businesses that replicate what they already do? Or is it venturing into new industries? The risk is lower with the former.

Still, you want the company to explore new markets and businesses. But take careful note of how they do it.

Focus on quality

Barber discusses the importance of having a clear vision about how to deliver shareholder value. That vision should be based on a sensible mathematical model as a reference to guide your decisions. We went over a basic mathematical model earlier while discussing ROIC and reinvestment.

At Halma, one key aspect of this model was the return on capital employed. It took them about five years to achieve a 40% return on capital employed, but once they reached it, they were never below that level and were reluctant to relinquish it.

Today, the focus is "return on total invested capital," or ROTIC. One of the joys of reading Halma's annual reports is finding that this return is a focus for the company. They discuss it and track it, which is part of their incentive compensation. Here is a chart on the following page from the annual report of 2024/2025:

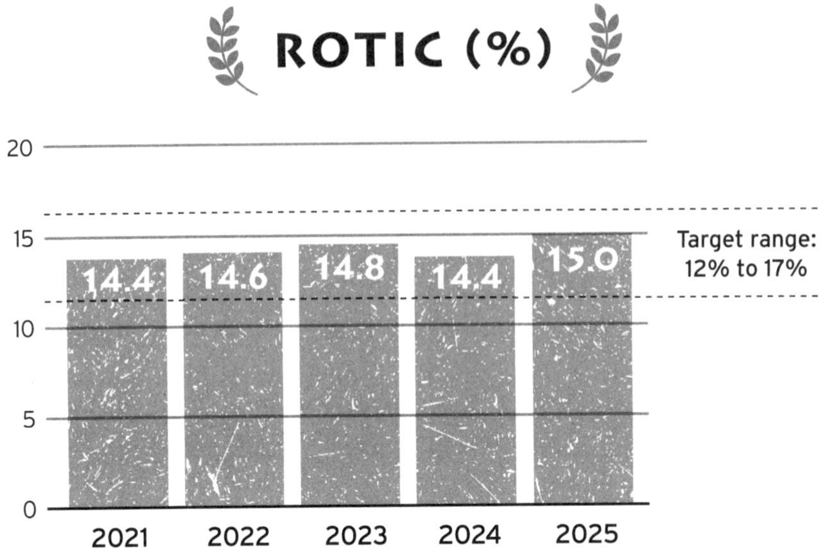

But this is not all. The company tracks return on sales, cash conversion, organic growth, and more in the same fashion. How refreshing — I wish more companies would do this kind of thing. When you find a company making these kinds of disclosures, pay attention.

When Halma makes an investment, it wants to ensure that its return at least meets what the company does now. As Barber says, the focus should be on quality, not on the deal's price. "It's an old saying, but a true one, that you can never pay enough for a good acquisition and never pay too little for a bad one." This is similar to how I think as an investor when looking at my own portfolio. Whatever I buy has to be better than whatever I sell, viewed primarily through the lens of ROIC and reinvestment, not price alone.

Barber provides a simple example to illustrate why, which I'll modify slightly. Imagine you run Microsoft and it is trading for a price-earnings ratio of 40x. You have the opportunity to acquire a homebuilder with a price-earnings ratio of 12x. The price looks attractive. If you sell part of Microsoft to finance the purchase, the math dictates that you will see an increase in earnings per share. And if it's a big deal, you'll see a big increase. But, do you have a better company after the deal? No, you've taken a great business and diluted it by adding a much inferior one.

To summarize, here are some basic things you might look for to find the next Halma:

- Share counts that don't increase much (or at all) over time
- Acquisitions using internally generated cash flow
- Acquisitions in the same or similar businesses
- A focus on quality (i.e., returns on capital)

TOP TAKEAWAYS

1. *Capital allocation, or how a firm decides to deploy its profits, is an important consideration.*
2. *On dividends: Ideally, we want companies to reinvest at high returns; any dividend is a leak that slows the compounding of capital.*
3. *Contrary to widespread misconceptions, acquisitions can generate substantial value for the acquirer.*
4. *One example we explored, Swedish serial acquirers, show where smaller programmatic acquisitions have created big winners.*
5. *Another example: Halma, demonstrates the importance of avoiding share dilution and focusing on business quality.*

CHAPTER 7

The Best Investors of All Time

The First Rule of Compounding

> "Compound interest is the eighth wonder of the world" (Einstein); **never interrupt it unnecessarily**" [bold added]
>
> — *Charlie Munger*

IT IS EASY to forget, because Odysseus's journey is filled with incidents: the Lotus-Eaters, the Cyclops, Aeolus, et al. The way home took 10 years, and this after 10 years of fighting in the Trojan War. His entire odyssey, then, took 20 years.

Think of the route home. Between those action scenes pass days and days of sailing on a featureless sea. It must've felt like the ship scarcely moved at all as the crew looked out at the empty horizon. Progress seemed invisible until, after years of pushing onward, the familiar shores rose out of the mist.

Compounding capital is a lot like this. For years, it can seem as if you are going nowhere fast.

Yet, everyone seems to acknowledge the power of compounding. The math is undeniable. If you earn 20% per year for 25 years, you'll wind up with about 100x your money, the coveted 100-bagger. But people forget that the math of this is heavily back-end loaded. After 20 years, you have ~38x. After 10 years, about ~6x. (See table in Chapter 3).

So, you don't want to interrupt that compounding lightly, as Munger advises. You'd better have a compelling reason to sell a winning business, not just because the stock doubled in a year and looks "expensive." Otherwise, your sale will look costly years later.

Even selling some, what's called trimming or rebalancing can cost you a lot of time. Trimming sounds so sensible. It satisfies that itch to *do something*. Yet, if you own an excellent business and take the long view, you're probably better off leaving it alone.

Another similar idea to trimming sounds smart, but doesn't hold up if you're a long-term investor. It goes like this: "X stock is too expensive; I need a 10% [or 20%] correction before I buy."

If you're a long-term investor, 10% or 20% is a rounding error.

Let's say I find a business I like. It checks all my boxes. The stock is $10 today, and I think it will be worth $50 in a decade. But, shucks, my buy price is sitting at $9 or $8. So, I'm just waiting for it to hit my buy price.

Does that sound wise? What would Munger say?

If my potential return is such that paying $8, $9, or $10 is the make-or-break on whether I buy it, I tell myself to look for a better idea. Again, I'm speaking from the perspective of a long-term owner of businesses. And I don't have to own many; 10-12 will do. If you're flipping stuff, the difference between $8 and $10 is the difference between eating and going hungry, so to speak. But if that's how you invest, you're probably not reading this book.

The Best Investors of All Time

We started our journey by considering what makes a good investor. The story about the lady from Nantucket aims to challenge a narrow conception of what a good investor looks like. If asked who the best investors of all time are, you probably would think of Warren Buffett, Peter Lynch, John Templeton, or other renowned money managers, past and present. (Or maybe you'll now think about that lady from Nantucket. I always do.)

But would you think of the Walton family, the Rales brothers, or Jeff Bezos? Why not?

We tend to think of them as entrepreneurs. But they own stakes in public companies just like other investors. In this case, the public companies are Walmart, Danaher, and Amazon. The returns on these stocks have been ... well, they would be the envy of nearly any traditional money manager you care to name.

Let's think about Sam Walton for a moment. He opened the first Walmart store in 1962 at age 44 (then called Wal-Mart). In 1970, he took the company public. The IPO generated nearly $5 million, which may not seem like a significant amount today. The Walton family retained about 60%, which put the overall equity at about $13 million. The Walton family stake was worth about $8 million.

By 1985, a mere 15 years later, Sam Walton was the wealthiest man in America, per *Forbes* magazine, with a net worth of $2.8 billion. So, $8 million to $2.8 billion in 15 years — a 350-bagger since the IPO. He stepped down as CEO in 1990 and died two years later, with an estimated net worth of $25 billion, representing a 10-fold increase from 1985. (I'm being a little casual about what's Sam's and what's Walton family money, but I don't think it matters much for the point I'm trying to make.)

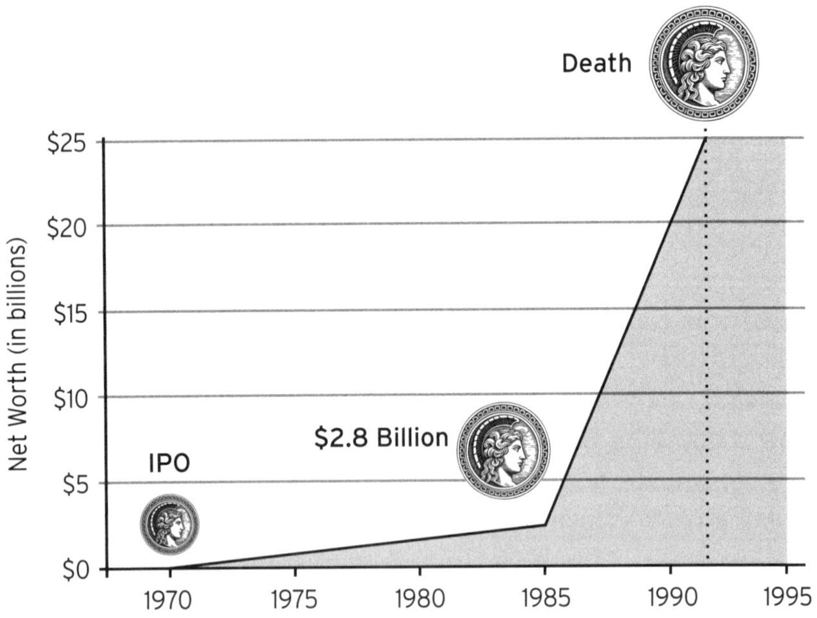

Fantastic returns. How did he get them? Essentially, he owned a great business, and he didn't sell it. Why can't we do the same?

A talk by Mohnish Pabrai, the founder and portfolio manager of Pabrai Funds, inspired the thoughts above. In it, Pabrai discussed Nicholas Sleep, who managed Nomad Investment Partners from 2001 to 2013, earning a net annual return of 18%. Pabrai recommended his letters, which I second.

Pabrai mentioned that Sleep told him the best investors were entrepreneurs who kept stock in their businesses. If we want the best returns, why not adopt the same approach as these individuals? Why bother with economists, Fed watchers, sell-side analysts, and quarterly earnings? Why bother with "taking profits," "trimming the position," and the like?

I love this message and have discussed and written about it myself. In *100 Baggers,* I note how many of these great stocks also have a person's name attached to them that is almost synonymous with the business. All I have to do is drop the name, and you can think of the company. (I say "Bill Gates," and you say ...)

Yet, as Pabrai pointed out, no professional investor held Walmart from the IPO to 1985. We don't know for sure; perhaps somebody did. But the point is that the vast majority did not. Many investors bought and sold Walmart over that time frame. Indeed, they would've been better off just sitting on the stock, as the Waltons did.

A story published by Dom Cooke in Colossus gives a real world example of this. Curran Harvey, was a portfolio manager for T. Rowe Price. He managed the New Horizons fund for a decade, whose focus was smaller, growth companies. In 1970, Harvey met Sam Walton and later bought a stake in Walmart at its IPO. For that decade Harvey managed the fund, Walmart increased its store base from 36 to 276. The stock compounded at 36% annually and became one of the largest holdings in the fund.

Harvey's successor was Jack LaPorte. He would go on to run the fund for 22 years and compile a remarkable record in which he beat the S&P 500 Index by four percentages per year. However,

LaPorte sold this Walmart stake.

LaPorte was followed by Henry Ellenbogen. If LaPorte had left the Walmart stake alone, it would have been worth more than the entire $8 billion that Ellenbogen inherited. "In other words," Cooke notes, "every good decision made by this procession of legendary investors over the course of half a century could not make up for the one cataclysmic mistake of selling Walmart prematurely."

Sleep wrote about this seeming inability of most investors to hang on to Walmart in his letter:

> "Investors are broadly rational people (they all knew that Wal-Mart was a wonderful business), and fund managers operate under healthy profit incentives that ought to foster good outcomes, *so why is it that no one but the founding Walton family owned Wal-Mart all the way through?*" [my emphasis]

What a great question. Reflecting on this question unlocks a wealth of investing wisdom.

First, we have to acknowledge that there are many possible answers. One reason may be that many investors thought they were doing the right thing by selling when Walmart seemed expensive and reinvesting the proceeds in less expensive and more attractive businesses. Sleep mentions this.

Investors frequently get this calculus wrong, and getting it wrong with a stock like Walmart is a catastrophic error as far as returns go. Any sale for any reason was a mistake, barring some urgent or unavoidable need to tap the funds.

In his letter, Sleep tells us how to avoid this mistake. I can't say it any better:

> "It could be argued that lots of things had to go right for Wal-Mart to grow for forty years. That is certainly true, but at its heart, *a very few simple things really mattered.* In our opinion, the central engine of success at Wal-Mart was a

> thrift orientation fueling growth with the savings shared with the customer. The culture of the firm celebrated this orientation and reinforced the good behavior. This is the deep reality of the business. This should have had the greatest weighting in the minds of long-term investors even if other things looked more important at the time. Instead investors may place too much emphasis on valuation heuristics, or margin trends, or incremental growth rates in revenues or any of the list above, but these items are transitory and anecdotal in nature." [my emphasis]

"A very few simple things really mattered ...", which reminds me of Sosnoff's minimalist art. And yet, to sell, investors must've focused on all kinds of things that didn't matter over the long haul. As he said, investors were paying too much attention to items "transitory and anecdotal in nature." Yes.

The answer to Sleep's great question seems to be that investors put too much weight on factors a business owner does not. A business owner seems to have a different set of concerns. A business owner is focused instead on the "central engine of success" of the business and the culture that keeps it alive and thriving.

It's best to leave the business alone as long as it continues to generate strong returns on capital and seems likely to do so for years. You want to invest as much capital as possible in these businesses.

Investing this way requires a complete change in mindset for most people, which explains why fewer investors have 100-baggers to their credit. I live in a glasshouse on this topic. It has taken me more than a quarter of a century to get here. That's years of reading, reflecting, and making mistakes. I have many scars. But I am ten years older than Sam Walton when he opened that first Walmart. There is plenty of time yet.

Anyway, part of that mindset change means a complete shift in how you filter, process, and evaluate information. Look away from the economic forecasts, quarterly earnings guesses, precise valuation models, charts, and news. Instead, figure out the "very few simple things" that matter, and focus on those.

Unlike business owners, we have one major advantage, we can own more than one great business. We can create a portfolio of great businesses. We can buy a dozen and let them run. We can be wrong about a bunch and still get an excellent result.

If you are a business owner already, you have a better sense of how to behave as an investor in public equities than people who have never owned their own business. Pabrai mentioned how he entertained no offers for a piece of the general partnership of his own money management business. That's his business. He never considered selling it, even when people approached him with an interest in buying a piece. He just said no. He knows it's an excellent business and believes it will be worth a lot more in the future.

I left corporate banking in 2004 after a 10-year career. I once had a customer who owned a business he could have sold for a significant amount to a regional acquirer. I sometimes wondered why he didn't take the money and be done with it. But now, years later, I understand. He knew the number was not enough. He would be giving it away. He understood the central engine of his success and was confident it had many years to run. He was right. Years later, I saw he finally sold. It was for a number that would've been unimaginable 15 years earlier.

The power of compounding. We investors talk about it a lot, but the great entrepreneurs, with their unshakable ownership stakes in outstanding businesses, really reap the rewards. We should strive to emulate them.

Trade for Show, Hold for Dough

You've probably never heard of S. Allen Nathanson (1911-1982). He was born in Toledo, Ohio, to an immigrant family of modest financial means. But starting in the 1930s, he began a lifelong study of stocks and built a fortune. When he died in 1982, he left an estate worth $10 million (or about $33 million in 2025 dollars).

Much like our lady from Nantucket and our founder-investors, Nathanson had a simple approach of buying good companies and holding on. A friend of his, Dave Seidenfeld, collected Nathanson's writings in a book titled *Bullishly Speaking*. It is worth highlighting here as another testament to the power of playing the long game, from a complete unknown who wound up rich:

> "Buying into good growing companies and having the willpower and patience to hold one's position over a long period of time permits the magic of compound growth to come into play; the results that can be attained are almost unbelievable."

Nathanson wrote a series of columns from 1966 to 1973 (with a few articles in 1980). The columns are quirky and digressive and sometimes feel dated, but they were always well-written and, at times, even witty. The investing wisdom is timeless.

Nathanson firmly believed that the best way to make big money in the markets is to invest in quality companies and hold on. (As he liked to say, "Trade for show, hold for dough.")

But as he says, no matter how much you read or are told about it, you won't become sold until you have "an experience."

A mystical visitation by the investing gods? A thunderbolt to the brain that finally made him give up on trading low price-to-book stocks?

The experience Nathanson refers to is holding a stock for many years and seeing it rise to multiple times more than what you paid.

To wit: You buy a stock that trades at a reasonable multiple, thinking it might increase earnings per share by 12% annually. Over the next seven years, through peaks and valleys, the stock more or less winds up where you thought it might. You double your money — slow work, yet a nice result.

You keep holding it. Then, earnings growth picks up a bit over the next seven years, and the multiple expands. At the end of fourteen years, you find a stock that trades for 8-12 times what you paid.

That is an extraordinary result, but it took a long time. It involved an extended period, which — let's be honest — seemed dull, much like the seemingly endless days on the open sea must've seemed to Odysseus and his crew. And you had to sit on your hands despite many stocks zipping by yours. You had to do nothing, even as the headlines of the day — the siren songs of finance — implored you to do something.

Nathanson puts great emphasis on having such an experience. He's had it happen enough times to write that "There is no greater thrill in the stock market." You realize that those who pay too much attention to the daily ups and downs of stock market prices have chosen a much more challenging, perhaps even an impossible, road to success in the marketplace.

People can learn these principles before they have such an experience, but it certainly helps to have it happen to you or a close relative. (Your grandmother, who left her Walmart shares alone for thirty years).

Another critical aspect of Nathanson's experience is how you can make a substantial amount of money in a stock that compounds at what seems a modest rate. If I told you about a stock growing 12% per year, you are unlikely to get too excited. However, over ten years, you'll make three times your money; over 20 years, you'll make ten times your money. Not bad at all.

I am reminded of Brown & Brown, the insurance broker that you've met a few times in this book. I loved the high insider ownership (mainly via the Brown family), the resilience (in the crisis year 2008, sales declined 1%), and the business's steady, cash-generating nature. But it was not a sexy grower. When I added it to Woodlock House's portfolio on opening day in January 2019, my expectations were relatively modest.

In my notes, I wrote that I'm "buying a high-quality, low-risk business for a fair price. ... Over the long haul, we should earn ~10%+ annually from here."

Return on equity in the prior years was 10-15%, and I thought my return would be in that ballpark. It doesn't sound extraordinary, but from the initial price of around $26 per share, the stock rose to over $100 per share in my sixth year of ownership.

The business improved. Over the six years, the return on equity increased steadily from approximately 12% to 18%. Brown & Brown expanded significantly into Europe, extending the runway for growth. But if I had told my investors I expected a four-bagger from Brown & Brown in six years, I wouldn't have sounded credible. Certainly not all of my ideas work out so well. The reverse happens, too, and companies can underperform expectations.

So, again, to Nathanson's point, all you had to do was buy and hold on to enjoy the magic of compounding. It helps to hold on, though, when you know your business is well-defended against competitors, which brings us to the subject of our next chapter.

TOP TAKEAWAYS

1. *Think about good investors more broadly so that you might reframe what you think good investors must do.*

2. *Consider founders as investors worthy of emulation. For example, Sam Walton became extraordinarily wealthy by owning a large number of Walmart shares and holding on to them.*

3. *We have much to learn from the behavior of these founders, who did what most public investors seem unable to do: sit tight with their ownership.*

4. *We also considered the experience of S. Allen Nathanson, a relatively unknown investor who made a fortune buying stocks and holding on.*

5. *Even modest returns pile up over time.*

6. *We looked at Brown & Brown as an example of a good company that surprised to the upside. However, you had to leave it alone for six years to enjoy a fourfold return.*

CHAPTER 8

The Gates of Troy

ODYSSEUS SPENT 10 YEARS fighting the war against Troy, because the Greeks found its walls of sun-baked stone sheer and unyielding. Those walls were renowned for their strength, and legend said they were built by the gods.

But even before these seemingly insurmountable walls of Troy, eventually, the Greeks found a way, with deception. And here enters the Trojan horse of lore, a reminder that no defense is completely impregnable.

In investing lingo, "moats" are what we call defenses that keep competitors from replicating what your company is doing and eroding its high returns on capital. But as the story of Troy reminds us, an analysis of what makes your company defensible against the competition, and thus able to earn those high returns, is crucial. The usual competitive advantages include things such as "network effects," "low-cost advantage," "switching costs," and "mafia connections" (I kid.) But moats can be messier and sometimes harder to spot than these archetypes suggest.

Let's look at a couple of moats in the wild, that are perhaps less traditional, but yet powerful.

Invisible Moats

The moats in this section are invisible in a sense. They are akin to what Odysseus found among the Phaeacians; a hidden harbor, protected by mist, accessible only to those who knew the way. Competitors didn't attack it because they didn't even know it was there. But anytime you find a business with a long track record of success in a competitive field, you should search for that defense, or invisible moat. Old Dominion Freight Lines (ODFL), which we learned about in Chapter 4, is a good example of what I mean.

A friend of mine argued that ODFL has no competitive advantage. It operates in a crowded and competitive field, which does not bode well for long-term success.

For context, this discussion occurred in 2019. The stock was about $70 per share.

ODFL had been a wonderful compounder. As pointed out in its 2019 report, shareholders have enjoyed annual returns (including dividends) of 30.7%, 19.8%, and 30.2% for the previous three-year, five-year, and ten-year periods, respectively.

Its ROIC has improved from single digits a decade ago to more than 20% by 2019. The company operates in a market with many competitors, true. But it has continually taken market share. By 2019, it had risen to #2, behind only FedEx Freight. In 2018, ODFL won the Mastio Quality Award as the #1 National Carrier for the *tenth* straight year.

Yet, my friend was put off by the competition. What is it that ODFL does that another trucker can't do? There were lots of competitors. Where was the moat? At first glance, it was hard to see how ODFL could defend its business. And just to show he wasn't crazy, Morningstar agreed. They gave the company a "no moat" rating. Here is a snippet from Matthew Young's report on ODFL, which sounds definitive:

> "In our view, even the best operators (like Old Dominion) struggle to carve out a sustainable competitive edge via the key economic moat sources: cost advantage, intangible assets, switching costs, and network effect.
>
> "At first glance, it might appear that the high-fixed-cost nature of LTL operations should allow for enduring scale-based cost advantages, or perhaps benefits from superior

> internal processes that optimize line-haul and pickup and delivery efficiency. However, routines capable of maximizing productivity can be replicated by well-capitalized competitors over time, and scale economies have largely proved insufficient across the industry. The near bankruptcy of industry behemoth YRC Worldwide following the 2009 freight recession stands as a prime example."

Morningstar gave ODFL one measly star, the lowest possible rating, and assigned a fair value of $40, nearly half of its then current stock price.

However, a company with rising ROICs and a growing market share must have something that others find difficult to replicate. Young's YRC analog was not a good one because YRC was unionized. That proved a significant disadvantage. Over time, non-union shops had steadily gained a share at the expense of unionized competitors. And YRC's finances seemed perpetually in poor shape, with numerous debts and pension obligations. ODFL had a strong balance sheet with little debt and was non-union.

ODFL didn't seem to have a traditional moat that fit into one of the usual buckets. Instead, it seemed to have pieces from different buckets. Somehow, the whole adds up to a strong competitor, though one might not be able to tell by looking at its parts.

To start, I pointed to their physical network. As ODFL said in a presentation, "Since the beginning of 2010, we have invested $1.5 billion in service center additions and expansions — adding 27 service centers (a 13% increase) and increasing our door count by approximately 51%."

This is not easy to replicate and run as efficiently as ODFL does, even if you had $1.5 billion at your disposal and locations as good as ODFL's. The trucking business is nuanced. ODFL is a less-than-truckload (LTL) carrier, as I mentioned earlier. This means it consolidates smaller shipments onto a single truck. The service centers' loading and unloading must be efficient. It's much more of a service business than you might guess.

For a full truckload business, it's different. You only need one truck to start. You get the proper license. And then if you get contracts to fill your truck, you're in business. You take goods from point A to point B.

But LTL is different. You need a large fleet of trucks and service centers where you can break down loads mid-route. You're not hauling goods across the country, from point A to point B. You're covering shorter distances and stopping at multiple locations. There is a lot more coordination involved.

If you delve into ODFL, you find an ownership culture difficult to replicate. A blog post by Scuttleblurb in 2017 said:

> "The Congdon family has continuously run the company since ODFL's founding in 1934, retaining Board and management presence and a 13% stake in ODFL shares [John Congdon (Chairman; 4.3%); Earl Congdon (Executive Chairman; 2.7%), David Congdon (CEO; 5.8%)]... Two salesmen I spoke with a few years back had their entire 401(k)s in Old Dominion stock and conveyed that Old Dominion stock is widely held among rank-and-file employees. ODFL shares comprise over 20% of employees' 401(k) assets. A significant portion of service center managers' quarterly bonuses are directly tied to profitability and service levels. Old Dominion's employee turnover, at 10%, is the lowest I've come across in the industry and the labor force, unlike those of most LTL peers, is union free."

Is that not a moat of a sort? I call it an "invisible moat." An invisible moat does not seem to fit any of the traditional buckets, but leaves a trail of rising ROICs and increasing market share.

From those $70 in 2019 to 2 January 2026, the stock was up almost 130% trading around $160 per share, not quite the $40 fair value Morningstar gave it. (I didn't own it for that ride!) ODFL continued to win industry awards for its service and to increase its market share.

The Greatest Industry in the History of Mankind?

> "Insurance policies... are the most complex contract that you'll ever enter into without the help of a lawyer."
> — *Hyatt Brown, Chairman at Brown & Brown*

In our mission to find great businesses to own, I offer another unusual and perhaps off the beaten path example, commercial insurance brokers.

As mentioned earlier, Brown & Brown is an insurance broker for businesses. Because a business's insurance needs can be complex and bespoke, insurance brokers play an important consultative role with their customers. Relationships are essential, and customers are sticky. Since every business needs insurance, the brokerage business is resilient even during economic distress.

The more I learned about Brown & Brown, the more I liked it and the industry it is in. John Wepler, Chairman of MarshBerry (a leading investment bank for the insurance brokerage industry), said in 2022:

> "The good news is that regardless to [sic] what happens to valuations, MarshBerry firmly believes that **insurance brokerage is the greatest industry in the history of mankind.**" [bold added]

Wepler may be overstating his case, but I sympathize with his enthusiasm. All of the publicly traded insurance brokers — not only Brown & Brown, but Aon, Marsh, and Arthur J. Gallagher — have performed well over a long period of time; they have posted market-beating returns for decades.

Of these, Brown & Brown is a good fit for my partnership with its high insider ownership (around 25%), anchored by the Brown family. However, employees are also significant owners, as I pointed out earlier. Hyatt Brown, in a talk from which I drew the quote above, emphasized the importance of employee ownership to him. In the early days, he established a plan whereby employees — teammates in Brown & Brown parlance — could purchase the stock at a 10% discount.

Many employees have taken him up on the offer, and they have made themselves rich over time. Here is a chart from Brown's talk:

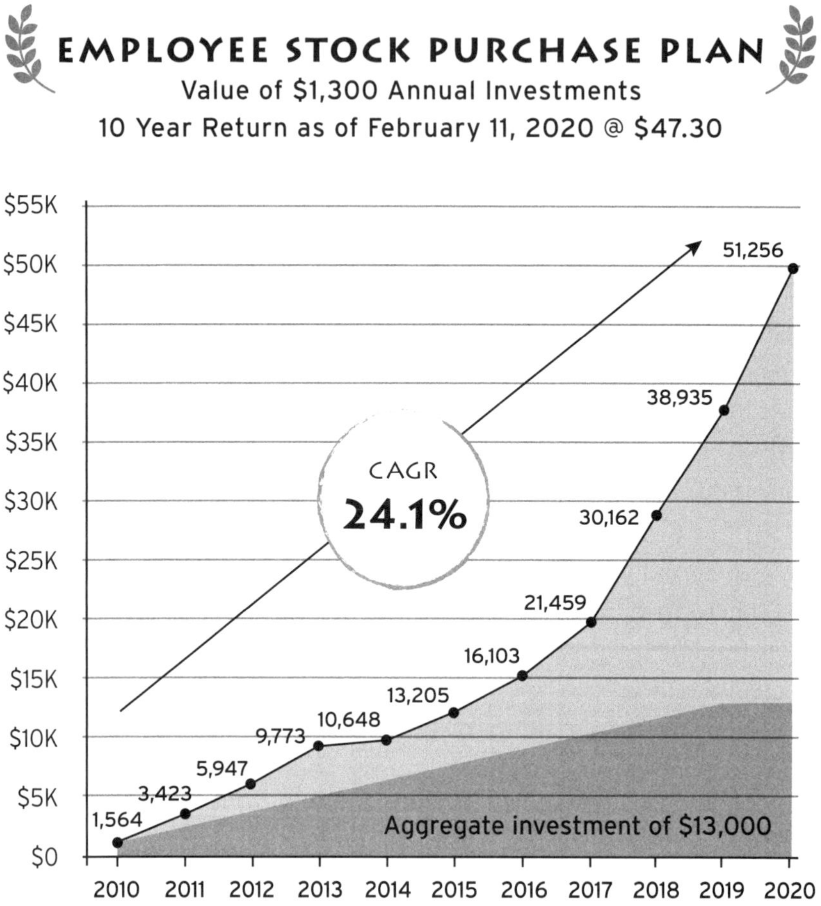

This is the hallmark of a good culture and reflects well on Brown's management. Preserving this culture is essential, and management frequently discusses it. The most significant risk to any insurance agency is losing its good people.

In addition to retaining good people, all publicly traded insurance brokers supplement their growth by acquiring more good people via acquisitions. As a result, the industry has undergone massive consolidation over the years.

Of the top 10 from 1972, only Marsh is still independent; the others have been acquired. Brown & Brown is now among the top six; revenues 2025 were almost $6 billion. Marsh remains the giant, with $27 billion in revenues. Aon is at $17 billion. While Brown has plenty of room to grow, the big heavies may be hitting some limits.

In 2021, the U.S. government blocked a merger between Aon and Willis Tower. Although the particulars don't interest me, I read the legal briefs and was struck by the discussion of these firms' competitive advantages.

To wit, the government used the CEO's own words against him, citing Willis Towers' annual report from 2018, in which he wrote, "High barriers to entry, existing market share, brand recognition and long-term client relationships give incumbents the edge over newcomers."

Further, the government noted, "the prevalence of post-employment non-compete and non-solicit clauses in the insurance broking industry, including by Aon and WTW, serve as barriers to attracting clients away from the Big Three (Aon, Marsh, and Willis Tower)."

Finally, and my favorite part, the government cited the failure of competitors to break through those barriers:

> **"Past attempts have shown that successful entry is difficult.** For example, several years ago a number of employees from one of the Big Three attempted to start their own commercial risk broking firm with a focus on serving large customers.
>
> "Despite having deep experience in the industry and existing relationships with many potential customers, this new venture failed to take much business from Aon, WTW, and Marsh.

> "Similarly, at least one major direct-to-consumer provider spent several years attempting to expand into the private multicarrier retiree exchange market, but has since abandoned that effort due to a lack of success. This direct-to-consumer provider's foray into private multicarrier retiree exchanges was hampered by, among other things, its lack of reputation and experience with large employers that Aon and WTW have handled for years."

The circuit court filing runs over 300 pages, but you get the gist. It affirms the competitive strengths of the established brokers. Now Brown is one-fifth the size of Marsh. Plus, Brown's acquisitions are usually small, but numerous. Brown did 43 during 2025. The company is still below the government's radar and has plenty of room to grow.

Still, it's interesting when the government makes the case for the competitive strengths of your business. Insurance brokerage may not be the greatest industry in the history of mankind, but it's pretty good.

TOP TAKEAWAYS

1. *Moats are what keep competitors from replicating what your company is doing and eroding its high returns on capital.*

2. *An invisible moat does not seem to fit any of the traditional buckets, but leaves a trail of rising ROICs and increasing market share.*

3. *We looked at Old Dominion as an example of a company with an "invisible moat."*

4. *We looked at insurance brokers as an example of an excellent business.*

CHAPTER 9

Playing the Long Game

MOATS THAT ENDURE become cultures that endure. Some last a century or more. What do they share?

Cultures seem to be "sticky." They are not easy to copy or change. As long-term investors, we're interested in longevity and things that last. What about the age of the business itself?

Companies don't last forever. They have lifespans, and those seem to be shortening. The average lifespan of a company on the S&P 500 has declined over time. According to a McKinsey report from 2023, the average lifespan of a company listed on the S&P 500 was 61 years in 1958. Today, it is less than 18 years.

This is not an exact science; different people will get different estimates. But the story here is directionally accurate.

Juxtapose this phenomenon against the median time it took for companies in my study to reach 100-bagger status, 26 years. (The mean was also about 26 years).

So, we see another aspect of our challenge, and it begs the question, what kinds of companies survive long enough to produce those wonderful multi-baggers?

The Century Club

Vicki TenHaken's book, *Lessons from Century Club Companies,* has some answers. The book focuses on companies that have been in existence for at least 100 years.

TenHaken became interested in these companies after hearing a presentation by Makoto Kanda, an economist who studied long-lived Japanese companies. Japan is home to some of the oldest continuously operating firms in the world, with seven founded before the year 1000. These are the bristlecone pines of the corporate world.

Fascinated, she turned to see how US companies fared. Corporate lifespans typically range from 12 to 15 years. Not many have joined the Century Club. In the US, over 1,000 companies have survived more than a century, a population of less than half of one percent of all companies operating today.

So, how did these companies beat the odds?

TenHaken's book seeks to answer this question. After ten years of work — conducting surveys, interviews, etc. — TenHaken presents the following model as the keys to the club:

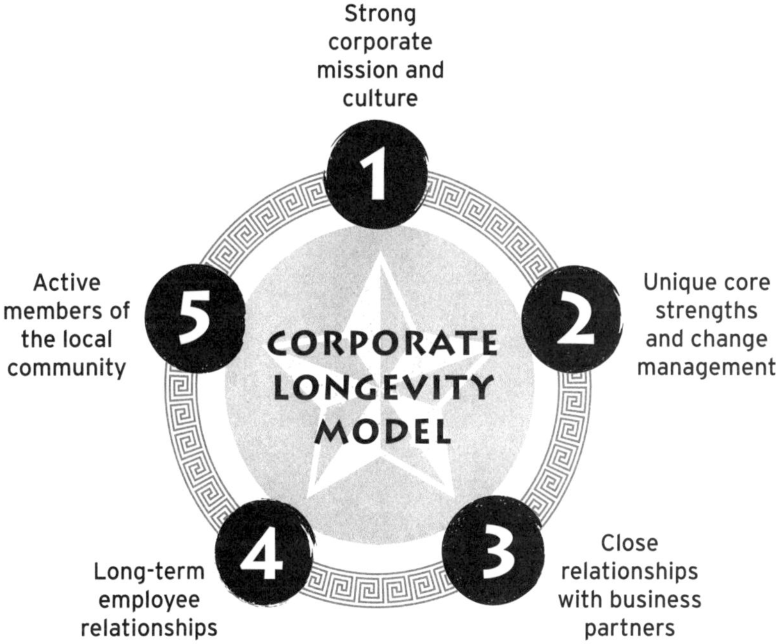

I'll share some highlights and thoughts on each below.

Strong corporate mission and culture

You have to figure that these keys will be intangibles that are hard to pin down, such as "culture." However, some elements are present that you can look for. For example, Century Club companies tend to be conservative financially; they don't use a lot of debt. They emphasize profitability over growth; TenHaken shows how century club companies tend to be highly profitable. In Japan, they are twice as profitable as their peers. In other countries, the gap is less pronounced but still significant.

Culture is also evident in other ways, such as consistently reiterating the company's purpose. "They talk about their purpose all the time," TenHaken writes of Century Club firms. Many companies seem to get this, at least based on my reading of annual reports, but perhaps more informative tells may come from management in less scripted settings. In any case, a strong sense of purpose appears to be a common element among Century Club members.

Unique core strengths and change management

"Century Club companies are not dinosaurs," TenHaken writes. Survival comes from a willingness to change and innovate.

TenHaken gives us many examples, such as the Jelly Bean Candy Company, established in 1898. The founding Goelitz family has a history of experimentation. The second generation made candy corn and buttercreams. The third and fourth generations made tangerine slices and spice drops. In 1965, they experimented by injecting different flavors into mini jelly beans. In 1973, they introduced Chocolate Dutch Mints. They didn't stop with jelly beans.

I can think of other, more extreme, examples. AO Smith, for example, began in 1874 by manufacturing metal parts for baby carriages and bicycles. Today, it makes water heaters, boilers, and filters. In between, AO Smith made steel frames for cars, vessels for the oil and gas industry, glass brewery tanks, and more. AO Smith also pushed out into other countries, such as China and India. That's a company that doesn't sit still. It has undergone several transformations over the course of its history.

So, Century Club companies don't rest on their laurels. They also tend to have offerings that are difficult to copy and a strong appeal other than price. These are things we naturally look for as long-term investors anyway.

Close relationships with business partners

Long-lived businesses tend to have long-lived relationships with suppliers and customers. So, Morse Lumber, established in 1853, has been doing business with Mascot Construction for 60 years, and both are proud to acknowledge the relationship. Armstrong, the flooring products company, has been doing business with Derr Flooring since 1918. Alden Shoe, established in 1884, has been getting its leather from Horween Leather Company, founded in 1905, since 1930.

An interesting question to ask the management teams of your favorite company is, what are some of your longest-running relationships with suppliers and/or customers, etc.?

Long-term employee relationships

Another simple one to suss out, which we discussed earlier. This is something I've asked about when researching companies if management doesn't mention it in their annual reports. When turnover is particularly low, management usually mentions it. I'll ask about the turnover of employees in different positions.

TenHaken says Century Club companies have long-tenured employees. She cites General Mills, founded in 1866. Although it has 16,000 employees, more than half of its workforce has been on the job for over ten years, with nearly 3,500 employees having been with the company for more than twenty years. That's incredible. There are many more examples.

Active members of the local community

Century Club companies tend to be rooted in their local communities, visible in their neighborhoods, and willing to contribute to various causes. TenHaken has, again, many examples. When an oil spill created a crisis in Marshall, Michigan, Schuler's Restaurant, established in 1909, fed over 2,500 clean-up crew members around the clock for months.

There are other ways this communal aid manifests itself. One interesting example is King Arthur Flour Company, founded in 1790, which pays its employees time off to volunteer with local nonprofits during work hours.

Century Club companies are also environmentally conscious. TenHaken says that half of the "Global 100 Most Sustainable Corporations in the World" are over 90 years old. So, there is another piece of evidence to look for.

These points are helpful and give you something else to consider when looking at which stocks you want to take with you on the long voyage to multi-bagger returns.

Also, if you invert everything, you get an intuitive picture of what won't last: companies having an ill-defined purpose with lots of financial leverage, low profits, lack of innovation, easy-to-copy products, short-term relationships with vendors and customers, lots of employee turnover and one that repeatedly turns the cold shoulder on its community.

Extinction & Survival

"Extinction is the rule. Survival is the exception."

— *Carl Sagan*

Century Club companies are the exception to Carl Sagan's rule. This leads to another key aspect of long-term investing that we must consider. It's so essential, yet many overlook it — simple survival. You have to prepare your businesses to survive potentially adverse conditions.

For example, let's look back at the 2020 pandemic, specifically the lockdown. There has been much talk about how the pandemic accelerated many already existing trends. One such trend is the shift from physical retail to digital commerce. Another trend could be the increasing number of people working from home instead of in an office.

However, the lockdown also created a new environment for many businesses, such as restaurants. Nobody included shutting down for 30 days in their business plan. Old economic models may not be able to survive such adjustments. For example, those models depend on diners being packed in at the restaurant, rather than those that can adapt to delivery or carryout.

Many businesses can die simultaneously or over a short period, just as in a biological extinction event. Bubbles that pop and leave a trail of bankruptcies. Or when governments change the rules of the game severely and suddenly, forcing companies to scramble to adjust or go out of business.

Surviving Prohibition

One of my favorite stories along these lines is how Anheuser-Busch survived prohibition in the 1920s. Murray Stahl tells the story in his book *How They Did It: Exceptional Stories of Great Investors*. The government made it illegal to sell beer. That is a big problem for a brewer.

But they did survive. First, they tried to make different products. Ice cream, for example. And non-alcoholic beer. The company refunded the latter effort if you could taste the difference. Most people couldn't. But they still didn't buy the beer, which tells you something.

Anyway, none of these worked. However, management eventually figured out a response that saved the company. They saw a loophole in the law. You couldn't make, sell, or transport alcoholic beverages. Okay. But it didn't outlaw the making, selling, and transporting of unfermented malt extract, which customers could then take home and use to brew their beer by adding water and allowing it to ferment. This is what Anheuser-Busch did; they began selling malt extract.

Soon, they were selling 6 million pounds annually, which can make an enormous amount of beer. August Busch said, "We ended up being the biggest bootlegging supply house in the United States."

Reflecting on this bit of history, Murray Stahl wrote how it humbles the short seller because it shows how "companies, if they are well capitalized, can be very resilient."

Being well-capitalized alone, though, may not be good enough. As we saw with the McKinsey study mentioned earlier, the average lifespan of companies listed in Standard & Poor's 500 has fallen to less than 18 years.

That's for the set of the biggest and often best-capitalized public companies on the market. I imagine the attrition rate is much higher in the Russell 2000, which comprises smaller companies. Or even worse, among private companies, where you've got many mom-and-pop businesses without easy access to capital.

Attributes of Survivors

Even in the most devastating events, there are survivors. An article published in *Aeon* by Renée Duckworth, an associate professor at the University of Arizona, is relevant to this discussion. She writes about the most famous mass extinction on Earth. More than half of all life perished when an asteroid hit the Yucatán Peninsula. But that means less than half survived. The catastrophe drove evolutionary change. "Survival required ingenuity and flexibility," she writes.

The same is true for companies. If Amazon had never branched out beyond selling books, it probably would not have survived as an independent company. If Apple doesn't create iPods and iPhones, etc., it probably won't survive. (a credit to having a creative genius as an owner-operator in Steve Jobs) Survival is more than being well-capitalized. You need that flexibility and ingenuity. Even so, financial strength is important and so I avoid companies with significant debt or those that rely on regular access to credit.

One rule of thumb in identifying excessive debt is that net debt should be less than two times EBITDA. If you agree with this, you'd rule out banks, REITs, and many other businesses right away. I'm okay with that. As mentioned in our upcoming chapters on portfolio management, you need some way to filter the vast universe of investing possibilities. And that means you'll intentionally turn a blind eye to big chunks of the market. Businesses that require significant leverage to generate a good return on equity are typically not the best investments. I'd rather stick with higher-quality businesses, but even high-quality ones can get into trouble with too much debt.

To ensure survival through whatever the market can throw at you requires redundancies, like layering on extra support and strength to a bridge or a wall, which seems excessive in normal circumstances. We're not worried about normal circumstances (whatever "normal" means); we're focused on survival, even during abnormal times.

A final note on survival is that you also need a bit of luck. Let's be frank about this. There are some risks in life we cannot escape.

The Quest for Better Explanations

Survival means the ability to solve problems. I've mentioned owner-operators and their creative role in guiding their companies to new markets. But there are also structural advantages to look for. There are ways of doing business that allow for course corrections.

To think about this, I'll refer to David Deutsch's *The Beginning of Infinity: Explanations that Transform the World.* It is not about finance or investing — Deutsch is a physicist — but a book where I kept finding interesting parallels to why investing with owner-operators is beneficial and how they correct for errors and/or solve problems.

Deutsch writes about human progress in understanding how the world works in a novel way, describing it as a quest for better explanations. For example, our knowledge of our solar system has improved from Ptolemy to Kepler to Newton. We have better explanations now.

But what makes the process of creating better explanations work? At its heart, Deutsch says, is a culture of criticism. We make bold conjectures about how things work, and then those conjectures are subject to testing and criticism.

Why is that important? Because it allows us to discount inadequate explanations and correct errors as we go along. If this sounds a bit like Karl Popper, it's because Popper had a definite influence on Deutsch.

As a result of this constant revision, we should be humble about how we think about ideas. We need to evaluate them in a way that takes into account this revision process. Here is a passage from Deutsch's book that I particularly liked:

> "So there is no resource management strategy that prevents disasters, just as there is no political system that provides only good leaders and good policies, nor a scientific method that provides only true theories. But there are ideas that reliably *cause* disasters. ... The only rational policy, in all three cases, is to judge institutions, plans, and ways of life according to how good they are at correcting mistakes: removing bad policies and leaders, superseding bad explanations, and recovering from disasters."

This is a rational way to judge a management team. Ask how well they correct mistakes and recover from disasters.

An Example: The Europium Crisis

To illustrate the idea of correcting errors as we go along, Deutsch tells a great story about europium. In the 1970s, this element was crucial in the development of color television sets. Europium is one of the rarest elements on Earth. The known reserves could only support a few million more television sets … and then we'd all be watching black-and-white. Only the elites would have color, so the story went at the time.

The reason we're not all watching black and white TV is because color screens today are composed of liquid crystals made from other more common elements. They don't require a cathode-ray tube like older television sets. In short, they don't need europium. And even if they did, it wouldn't matter. Deutsch writes, "Now enough europium has been mined to supply every human being on earth with a dozen europium-type screens, and the known reserves of the element comprise several times that amount."

This is why I can never get excited about a resource depletion story. I don't care if it's oil, uranium, or rare earths. It's always the same story, and there are many such stories in financial history. As Deutsch says, such debates come down to a "contrast between two different conceptions of what people are." In the pessimistic scenario, people are merely consumers, mindlessly eating away at limited resources. In the optimistic one, they are problem-solvers who can create alternatives and new supplies.

Deutsch writes, "By casting problems in terms of resource depletion and ignoring the human level of explanations," we miss all the important determinants of what we're trying to predict, namely, "[Do] the relevant people and institutions have what it takes to solve problems?"

I like the underlying humility in the approach he advocates — one built on continued testing and revision of ideas. It's difficult to assess this with a business, but it's worth thinking about and investigating.

Owner-operators are Problem Solvers

One reason I like investing with owner-operators is they will own this problem. They are problem solvers, and they have a great incentive to be problem-solvers. They have skin in the game. Whether it's the Mendelsons at Heico or the Browns at Brown & Brown, they're all talented problem solvers.

As a passive, outside minority investor, I can't be there every day watching the store. I have to trust the management team to do that.

This reminds me of an interview with Warren Buffett:

> **Andy Serwer:** "Let's talk a little bit about Apple. … You have a 45 billion dollar stake, more or less. How closely do you follow the company?"
>
> **Warren Buffett:** "Well, if you have to closely follow a company, you shouldn't own it!"

That's funny, *and* wise. Investing demands patience. And the ability to net a big multi-bagger hinges on your ability to hold on to a stock for many years. That's hard, but it's even more challenging if you're watching the company too closely.

My friend Ian Cassel wrote about the dangers of overthinking your positions. He advised, "Give them some room to breathe. There is some room to disappoint you, but still hold on. Some room to exceed your expectations but not sell."

I think that's a good course to sail between Scylla and Charybdis, and with the right team and incentives, you give them a chance to solve problems and overcome challenges. On the other side of it, the company may well emerge as a better company and a better investment for having gone through it.

Making these judgment calls requires that you know your business well. One way to help you get there is to study fewer businesses. We'll take a look at the counterintuitive benefits of a shrunken investment universe in the next chapter.

TOP TAKEAWAYS

1. *Corporate lifespans are shortening, while playing the long game is required for investors wanting to nab multi-baggers.*

2. *The Century Club — businesses that have been around for 100+ years — exhibit similar traits: a strong corporate culture, management willing to experiment, close relationships with business partners, long-term employees, and active members of their community.*

3. *Survival is the exception. Your businesses have to outlive crises.*

4. *The government made it illegal to sell beer; Anheuser-Busch adapted and survived.*

5. *Survival attributes include ingenuity, flexibility, capital, and limited debt.*

6. *We looked at the value of owner-operators as problem solvers who correct errors and overcome challenges.*

CHAPTER 10

The Investable Universe Shrinks

AFTER READING TO this point, you probably won't be surprised to hear that the more I learn about businesses, the more I find my investment universe shrinking.

It seems counterintuitive at first. If you spend a lot of time studying businesses worldwide, you'll think your circle of competence will widen over time, and you will find more ideas, not fewer.

In my experience, it doesn't work that way. As you get pickier over time, your checklist grows longer. Thus, the list of companies that check all those boxes starts to get shorter.

I always marvel at these funds, which say they have investable universes of hundreds of names. Gosh, I have a hard time finding ten companies I love. I exaggerate, but not much. As 2026 begins, I have 12 stocks in my portfolio, and I'd be hard-pressed to name 10 more that I'd love to own at the right price.

Pickiness is suitable for the long-haul investor. If you buy something you are less than enthusiastic about, you are unlikely to hold it for long. You'll be too quick to chase the next shiny spinner that dances across your view. Worse, you will probably sell what you have at a bad time. And that new shiny spinner might have a nasty hook.

The Virtues of a Concentrated Portfolio

Being picky naturally leads one to own a concentrated portfolio. For the sake of discussion, let's say concentrated means portfolios with no more than 20 securities. The idea is you don't invest in many companies, but when you invest, you invest a sizable part of your portfolio. This is far from how most people manage money.

Many compelling case studies say focus is the way to go. I'd recommend *Concentrated Investing: Strategies of the World's Greatest Concentrated Investors,* by Allen Benello, Michael van Biema, and Tobias Carlisle. There are some incredible stories in there.

For example, Lou Simpson ran GEICO's portfolio from 1979 to 2010. His record is extraordinary: 20% annually, compared to 13.5% for the market.

Simpson's portfolio seemed to become more concentrated over time. In 1982, it contained 33 stocks in a $280 million portfolio. However, as the portfolio grew, Simpson kept reducing the number of stocks he owned. By 1995, it contained just ten stocks in a $1.1 billion portfolio.

A lesser-known example is Joe Rosenfeld at Grinnell College. When he took over in 1968, the endowment had $11 million in assets. When he stepped down in 1999, it was up to $1 billion. Rosenfeld delivered 15% annually, net of the 4.75% that went to the college every year.

He did it by buying a handful of stocks and holding on. In 30 years, he made half a dozen significant investments and sold even more rarely. Rosenfeld "considers selling to be indistinguishable from error."

Of course, this approach led to some harrowing moments. In 1990, the endowment dropped by a third, largely due to a giant position in Freddie Mac. But Rosenfeld held on.

Okay, so there are lots of anecdotes. What about empirical research?

A survey of some of that research by Lazard Asset Management says most research supports concentrated investing, but "the empirical results … are not unanimous."

I'm not sure there is a correct answer. My gut says that your success with a concentrated portfolio depends more on temperament than anything else. Concentrated portfolios tend to be more volatile. And if you can't stomach the ups and downs, it probably won't work for you.

But it begs another question.

How Concentrated Is Concentrated?

The number of positions is one thing. But that's not the only dimension here. How big do you let positions get? Because if you buy and hold and nab a big winner, you may get a nutty-looking portfolio after some years.

Say you took a 3% position in Intel in 1987 and never sold. Twenty years later, it could be your entire portfolio. Of course, almost nobody would allow this to happen.

In 2017, Murray Stahl wrote an essay titled "How Could Indexation Ever Be Invalidated?" (I took the Intel case from this, though I could've chosen many other examples).

Stahl wrote:

> "If the only assertion about indexation is that the index will outperform the active managers, then the only way to invalidate indexation is to outperform the index. *The index can be made to do anything except compound into heavy concentration.* This is an approach that the active manager might do well to explore." [my emphasis]

Since Stahl wrote this, the S&P 500 became so highly concentrated that by the end of 2025, the top three alone were more than 20% of the entire index. The top ten were around 40%. Further, there is no maximum cap on how big a company can get in the index. Historically, Stahl is right; the index tended not to be concentrated. Perhaps it's a small wonder that the index has had such a strong run since. From 2017 to 2025 the index generated a return of around 15% annually, well above its longer-term average of 10%. So Stahl's thesis holds, sort of. The index has beaten its own longer-run average by allowing itself to become more concentrated than historically.

I've been running concentrated portfolios my whole investing

S&P 500: WEIGHTING OF TOP 3 HOLDINGS

Annual (1980-2025)

Data Source: S&P Dow Jones as of 10/29/25

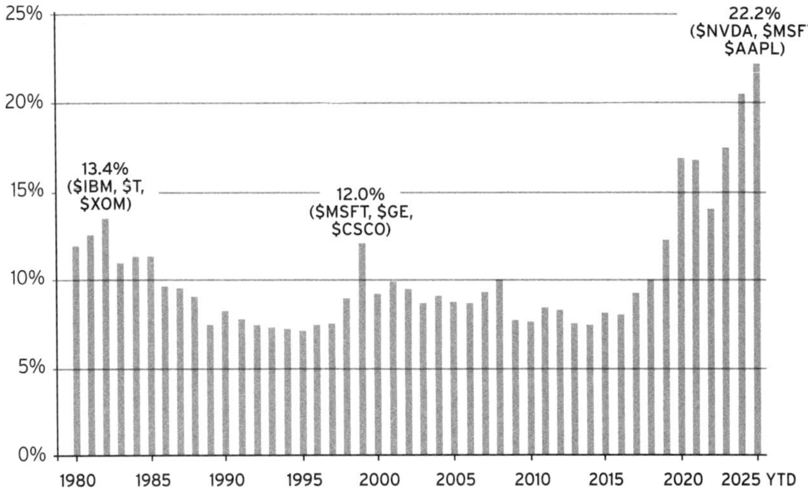

S&P 500: WEIGHTING OF TOP 10 HOLDINGS

Annual (1980-2025)

Data Source: S&P Dow Jones as of 10/29/25

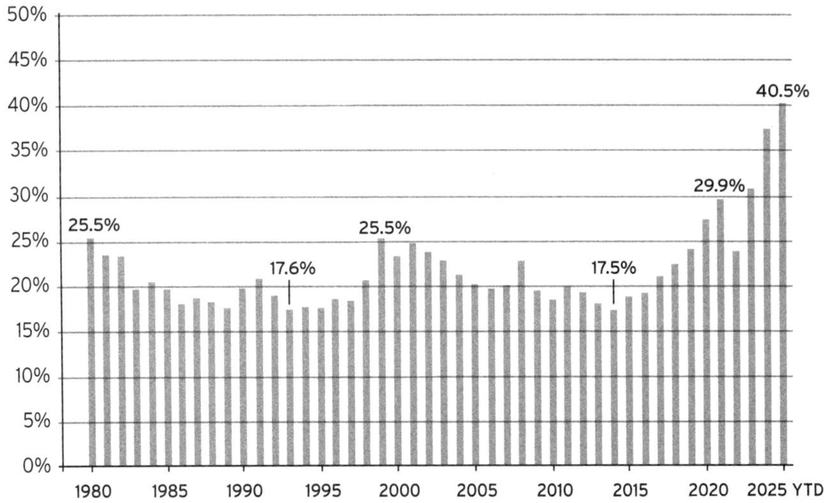

life. I'm sold, but not everybody is. I spoke with one fellow professional who told me that letting a position become 20% of the portfolio would be "financially irresponsible."

Would it? What if it started as a 3% position?

This is the conundrum of investors today. Everybody is watching the S&P 500 Index. They want to beat that index. But to beat that index means you must do things the index doesn't. One way to do that is to allow your portfolio to become top-heavy, chunky, or unbalanced. Choose your adjective.

However, not many people want to do that because it means suffering more stock price volatility. Everyone seems to want low volatility.

I like to start with a position size of 3-4%, depending on my familiarity with the company. Rarely will I push anything to 8% right away. Nothing wrong with starting small. You can always add more later as your conviction grows and as the business performs. Otherwise, I just let it run. In my fund, the limit for any position is 25%. I don't know what the right number should be. Maybe there shouldn't be a number. But we do make mistakes and bad things happen. My gut says you want a limit. You don't want your portfolio to die because you were wrong or surprised by one business going bad.

This reminds me of a quote from Nick Murray's wise little book *Simple Wealth, Inevitable Wealth*: **"The fewer ideas in your portfolio, the fewer bullets it will take to kill you. One idea: one bullet."**

Mindful of one bullet, I try to balance risks. I own companies in different industries that do business in different places worldwide. This is not a science; it is more using your intuition and your ability to suffer pain if you're wrong.

Moreover, such positions still must meet my investment criteria, which include a robust balance sheet. Certain styles are better suited to concentrated portfolios than others. For example, investors in small biotech firms or speculative mining companies should spread their dollars over a broader base of investments, because the risk of any individual firm in these spaces going to zero, or near zero, is pretty high.

The Secret to Success? Tennis Shoes!

I'll end this bit on concentrated investing with a funny story Glenn Greenberg, founder of Brave Warrior, tells. This story is in *Concentrated Investing.* Greenberg worked for a family office. The money manager there was a guy named Arthur Ross. He wasn't famous because he invested private money and kept a low profile. He didn't write books or talk to the media. But he was an outstanding investor.

One day, a family member came into Ross's office and asked, "Arthur, what's the secret of your success?"

Ross said, "Tennis shoes. Now get out of my office."

And the guy leaves and thinks to himself, "Tennis shoes? I don't get it." So he goes down the hall to the office of one of Ross's analysts and says, "Arthur told me the secret to his success is tennis shoes."

The analyst tells him that Ross said "ten issues". He owns ten issues — just ten stocks.

Maybe people are starting to understand this. In 2018, an article in *The Economist* cited data showing that the average number of stocks in global portfolios has halved over the past decade. But is ten the right answer?

How Many Stocks?

How many stocks in a portfolio are enough, not enough, or too many?

There are many ways to answer this question. I don't think there is an ideal answer for everyone. It's a matter of personal taste, psychology, and skill set. Below, I'd like to share how I think about the question.

First, owning more stocks will not necessarily save you. Many people seem to believe that if they own more stocks, they are "diversified." Owning fewer stocks is somehow "riskier" and "dangerous." But what is prudent can be quite the opposite (though there is an exception, which I'll get to below.)

Let me share a great story with you, as told by Joel Greenblatt, who credits Warren Buffett with the tale. Suppose you own a business and you sell it for $1 million. Now you have $1 million to invest. You want to figure out something smart to do with it.

So you look at all the businesses in your town. Let's say there are a hundred businesses. You start looking for businesses where the management is good, and the prospects of the business seem attractive. You see that it's well run, they treat employees right, and people seem to like working there.

After researching these businesses, you find eight that you like. You divide your million dollars among those eight businesses. As Greenblatt says, "no one would think that's imprudent. They would actually think that was pretty prudent."

But if you called those businesses "stocks" and you get stock quotes every minute of every trading day and they bounce around all over the place, now people might say you're not diversified enough.

The lesson is clear, "You did a lot of research and invested in eight different businesses with the proceeds of your sale. People would think you're a pretty prudent person. All of a sudden if you invested in [eight] "stocks" and did the same type of work, people think you're insane."

The most crucial point here is "you did a lot of research." It would be ridiculous to buy eight businesses without understanding them well. Most people can't dedicate the time and resources to studying businesses. So if you can't do that, you shouldn't buy individual stocks, at least not with serious money. You may be better off in a fund or index.

There is another important point that sometimes gets overlooked. If you want to run a concentrated portfolio, then certain stocks must be off-limits (for example, highly leveraged businesses), or you risk disaster. Your focus needs to be "Don't lose money." And you can do that by raising the quality of what you own. As Warren Buffett often said, search out wonderful businesses, and ignore everything else.

I've been watching old Berkshire meetings on YouTube. (It is addictive). In an excellent clip from the 1996 annual meeting where Buffett and Munger talk about diversification, Buffett said that if you want to be sure nothing terrible happens to you relative to the market, then you just own the market. That seems plain enough, and there is nothing wrong with that. If you don't want to spend a lot of time studying businesses, this is the prudent approach.

But if you want to study businesses and you learn how to analyze them and value them, then it's crazy to own 50 stocks, or even 30 stocks, for the simple reason that there aren't that many wonderful businesses around. Especially one that a single human being can understand. Moreover, Buffett points out that by owning stock number 30, for example, you are forgoing the chance to put more money in your number one, or even in your top five.

If you look at how people have made fortunes in the US, they didn't get there by building a portfolio of stocks. They owned one great business. The Walton family owned a lot of Walmart and stayed put. There aren't 50 Walmarts around. There aren't even 20. But you don't need that many wonderful businesses. You need very few.

Here is Buffett closing out the argument:

> "If you had a really wonderful business... very well protected against the vicissitudes of the economy over time...

> Three of those will be better than a hundred average businesses. And they'll be safer incidentally. **There is less risk in owning three easy-to-identify, wonderful businesses than there is in owning 50 well-known, big businesses.** It's amazing what has been taught over the years in finance classes." [bold added]

Everyone will have to find their answer to "how many stocks?" And there's more to think about than what I have addressed here.

I love owning no more than a dozen fantastic businesses that I get to know well and then leaving them alone. There is no trimming, "trading around positions," and no fretting during drawdowns. I just let the businesses be as long as they continue to perform.

The Elements of Portfolio Construction

I decided to search academic articles for information on this topic. While there is a wealth of material about valuing stocks and picking them, little is about the actual continuous running of a portfolio. I found various mathematical treatments in my search, but they seemed impractical. Then, I stumbled on a piece by Frank E. Block, "The Elements of Portfolio Construction," published in the *Financial Analysts Journal* in 1969.

I was sucked right in by Block's opening lines. He writes that building and running a portfolio are "among the weakest sectors of the literature of investing." Block says that, while there has been a lot written by mathematically oriented scholars, "the problem is that a general theory of continuous portfolio management has not yet evolved."

Confirmation bias? Probably. Anyway, I continued to read.

I know many revolutions around the sun separate us from 1969. However, what I like about Block's article is that his treatment of the issues seems timeless. He doesn't arrive at any magical answers. Nonetheless, I like the thought process, and you may find it helpful to review some of the "elements of portfolio construction."

Block himself was a CFA and a VP of a bank. He was a practitioner, but with one foot in the academic world as he was also the assistant editor of the *Financial Analysts Journal.* So, he comes at the subject with a good perspective from both camps.

He begins by noting the wide gaps between investors' and academics' thoughts.

How to Think About Risk

For example, take the idea of risk. For academics, "risk is measured by variability of rate of return, which they express in such familiar statistical terms as standard deviation, variance, semivariance, and so on." This hasn't changed since 1969!

For me, and I suspect most practitioners, risk is about earning a poor return. And so when I'm trying to gauge risk, I tend to focus on things that could impact long-term returns. I think about the financial leverage in the business. I think about its ability to generate cash. I think about the durability of the business itself. What kind of competition does it face? These are the things I focus on, not how much the price has bounced around.

This gap with academics here seems unbridgeable to me. And so, much of the academic literature on portfolio construction is a no-go because it starts with this fundamental assumption that volatility is a risk. If that's how you begin, you're bound to offer advice that's a non-starter for most investors.

Block says as much:

> "Occasionally, portfolio managers are startled to read an academic paper which seems to say that a particular mechanism may be used to accomplish something the portfolio manager is striving to avoid."

Diversification is one area where this comes out. Academics love diversification, but of a peculiar kind. Block gives us an example from William Sharpe, the inventor of the Sharpe ratio and one of the giants of academic finance. Sharpe wrote that "diversification enables the investor to escape all but the risk resulting from swings in economic activity. This type of risk remains even in efficient combinations."

However, most portfolio managers would not consider that the primary purpose of diversification. As Block says, an investor "does not wish to escape the unique characteristics of his portfolio holdings; he wants to participate in that uniqueness. That is why he purchased those particular securities."

Diversification, to me, is more about trying to mitigate unknowable events that could take me out of the game. As I've said, I hold 10-12 stocks. This strategy is not for everyone. You must be okay with the (likely) higher volatility. You also have to be careful about your selections. With a "tennis shoes" (10-stock) portfolio, there are many stocks I never even consider. As mentioned, I avoid financial leverage. ("I learned this very early," Peter Lynch once said. "It is very hard to go bankrupt if you don't have any debt.") Companies that don't generate free cash flow get a quick boot. Ditto turnarounds. ("Turnarounds seldom turn," Buffett wrote back in 1979). The list goes on.

How to Think About Diversification

So, according to Block, how many stocks should you own?

Block uses a basic probability exercise to determine the number of stocks one should have in a portfolio.

First, he makes some assumptions, among them:

- An investor picks three winners out of every 10.
- "Winner" here means it performs better than the market average.
- Of the remaining seven, six perform more or less in line with the market.
- And one is a loser.
- Further, one winner offsets one loser.

How many stocks should you hold if success means beating, or at least matching, the market?

Block presents the following table:

Probability of Success (%)	Number of Stocks in the Portfolio
90	15
95	25
98	38
99	49
99.9	86

Intuitively, that feels right. What might be surprising is how only 15 stocks give you a 90% chance of success. Of course, you could tweak his assumptions and get lower numbers, but it holds that you don't need as many stocks as you may think to get the job done. (The table makes a general point. Don't get too wrapped up in its precision just because there are numbers.)

But there is more. I didn't say over what time interval we measure such returns. Let's say it's one year or even five years. Either way, "the likelihood of [the 15-stock portfolio] being unsuccessful in two consecutive time intervals is only 1%, or a 99% success ratio."

Thus, the key takeaway, which Block emphasizes with italics, is that "The amount of diversification needed is a function of the time horizon."

Put another way: The longer your time horizon, the less need you have for diversification.

TOP TAKEAWAYS

1. *Being picky about what businesses you own naturally leads you to a concentrated portfolio.*
2. *There is plenty of evidence that owning 20 or fewer stocks is a winning path.*
3. *To beat the index you must do things the index rarely does, such as letting positions get outsized.*
4. *"The fewer ideas in your portfolio, the fewer bullets it will take to kill you. One idea: one bullet."*
5. *Do your research, require robust balance sheets, and own companies in different industries that do business in different places worldwide.*
6. *Even under modest success rates, investors only need 15 stocks for a 90% chance to beat the index.*
7. *The amount of diversification you need is a function of time horizon; the longer the time horizon the less important diversification becomes.*

CHAPTER 11

Sailing the Ship

ODYSSEUS AS THE captain of his vessel had to make many decisions along the way. A different captain with the same ship and crew, may well have a different outcome.

As it relates to investing, those decisions along the way fall into portfolio management, an under-appreciated skill that can turn a good investor into a mediocre one, and vice versa.

I was in St. Moritz, Switzerland, for MOI Global's Ideaweek in 2019. I enjoyed many of the presentations. One of them was by Elliott Turner, a co-founder and managing partner at RGA Investment Advisors in New York City, who delivered a talk on position sizing. (Position sizing deals with how much you put in each idea in your portfolio.)

Turner started with an interesting observation, and I'm paraphrasing here. He knows someone who is an outstanding analyst whose returns are mediocre because his position sizing is off. He also knows an average analyst who delivers good returns because he gets his position sizing right.

Considering these two, Turner reflected on how position sizing could be a core competence in delivering good returns. A lively discussion ensued, and many people had strong opinions on how to do this.

Turner asked if anyone knew of books on this subject or something worth reading. Surprisingly, there doesn't seem to be much out there. At least, it stumped our group.

One book that came up was Lee Freeman-Shor's *The Art of Execution: How the World's Best Investors Get It Wrong and Still*

Make Millions (2015). I read this book, and I have to say, it has a great premise.

Freeman-Shor was a fund-of-funds manager at Old Mutual Global Investors. (He managed a portfolio of other funds.) He ran an experiment that lasted seven years, from June 2006 to October 2013. He says it covered 1,866 investments and 30,874 trades made by 45 of the world's top investors.

He gave each of these 45 managers between $20 million and $150 million to invest in his "Best Ideas" fund. They could only invest in ten stocks that represented their best ideas.

The result of this experiment was fairly shocking. Only 49% of the best investment ideas made money. Even more shocking, some of these legendary investors were only successful 30% of the time. Yet, as Freeman-Shor reported, "what really fascinated me was the fact that, despite some of them only making money on one out of every three investments, *overall almost all of them did not lose money.* In fact, they still made a lot of it."

Naturally, the rest of the book is about how this happened. And, as you might've guessed by now, what allowed these investors to do this was all about position-sizing — how they navigated the ups and downs of their ideas.

For example, let's say you buy a stock at the start of the year. It drops 30%. And then it finishes the year back where it started. If you did nothing, your return would be 0%.

However, how you respond to that drop can dramatically change the outcome.

What if you bought more? If you doubled up after it fell, say, 20%, you would have earned an 11% gain on that position. Not bad. (I wonder if this matters much over the long run. The more critical skill seems to me is the one Thomas Phelps preached in *100 to 1 in the Stock Market*: buy right and hold on.)

What if you sold it quickly and invested it in something else? Some investors were successful in this. As Freeman-Shor says, they were quick to "kill" their losses.

There are different ways to do it, but in Freeman-Shor's

experiment, the better performers seemed to choose one of two options — buy more or sell out — when faced with a position going against them.

In another chapter, he looks at how investors deal with winning positions. Do they take small profits or let winners ride? The most successful investors in his experiment seemed to let winners ride.

What to Do Depends on Your Style

How you do this depends on your style and temperament. I've seen various methods that work well enough for different people.

As for me, I'm likely to buy more if a stock I own falls. I tend to own stocks with great balance sheets and insider alignment. So I can have confidence buying more if the stock falls.

It would be more challenging to behave this way if I invested in leveraged equities or stocks in which I could not trust the insiders to do the right thing.

I also start positions with room to buy more. I rarely get out of the gate with a full position, and I let winners ride.

I'm also okay holding a stock that doesn't go anywhere for a few years, as long as I'm confident that the value of the business is still growing and hasn't been impaired.

Ideally, I'd hold on to my stocks for years — five years, 10 years, etc. That's when you get the benefits of all tax-free compounding.

To do that, you have to be reluctant to make switches solely based on valuation. Again, think of the lady from Nantucket. Surely there were points along the way where Berkshire Hathaway looked expensive. Think how costly it was to sell shares then.

There are many problems selling one great business because you think it might be over-priced to buy another one you think is cheaper. You could be wrong about the stock you're selling. You could be wrong about the stock you're buying. You pay fees for trading and probably have to pay taxes on your gains. You might recall these arguments from my thoughts on trimming.

Further, as a friend of mine used to say, the most risky position in your portfolio is the newest one. It's the idea you know the least. It doesn't matter how much time you spent researching it; there is something about owning a position that cannot be replicated by just watching it. You know what you own better than what you don't. Ergo, favor what you already own and know.

Add all that together, and I have a basic rule of portfolio management. Any new idea must be *significantly* better than its predecessor.

I find businesses that might be better than I have, but not by much. For me to make a move, it's gotta be obvious. I think this is a good way to keep your portfolio trimmed up. Only replace when something is way better. Don't talk yourself into taking marginal upgrades. Keep that bar high. Stay concentrated, resist the sirens, and play the long game.

How to Think About Cash

Concerns over short-term portfolio performance can make you feel impatient. You know that cash can be a significant drag on your returns if you hold onto it for too long. And if you're behind in performance, the pressure to invest and *catch up* may be even more significant.

All of the above ties in with how you initially think about cash. Does it burn a hole in your pocket? Or are you okay holding cash? It's an important question to think about.

I always liked what Chuck Akre had to say about managing cash. Basically, he does not part with cash to "stay fully invested." He only parts with cash when there is something specific he wants to invest in:

> "We appreciate that cash compounds at a negligible rate. But we also believe cash can be an accelerant of long-term returns when it is reserved for 'highest and best' opportunities rather than sprinkled pro-rata up and down the portfolio. In short, we do not look at cash to determine whether

to buy stocks; we look at stocks to determine whether to deploy cash."

That's how I think about it. I don't want to invest just because I have the cash. I want the opportunity to drive the decision. So, I'm keeping the bar high, erring on that side of things rather than lowering the bar a bit to get the cash invested.

After all, I'm looking for businesses I can own for a decade and will deliver strong returns. I think it's okay if it takes me a few months of sitting on cash to make that commitment.

As with most things, moderation is good. If your bar is too high, you wind up sitting on cash and missing out on lots of good opportunities to put your cash to work. Remember our look at Mark Leonard and how he lowered his already high hurdle rates to put more capital to work? There is a balance.

As a practical matter, I don't usually have significant levels of cash (say 10% or more) unless I sell something, which doesn't happen too often (or shouldn't).

Investing Abroad

There is another portfolio question we should address. Should you invest outside your home market? This involves additional risks, some of which are obvious, while others are not.

I think of those now-famous lines from the late Donald Rumsfeld, "There are known knowns; there are things we know we know. We also know there are known unknowns; that is to say, we know there are some things we do not know. But there are also unknown unknowns — the ones we don't know we don't know."

Whatever you think of his politics, you must admit he made a wise observation here, and certainly applicable to investing. He added that "the latter category tend [sic] to be the difficult ones."

Investing in a market other than your home market entails more of the unknown unknowns.

For example, I always think of a story Murray Stahl told in his

1995 collection of essays, "Collected Commentaries and Conundrums Regarding Value Investing." The essay is titled "An Unorthodox View of Emerging Market Investing."

He begins by telling us about Hungary in 1994. It is an emerging market. Despite a problematic history, it is on "the verge of major economic progress." It has a stable democracy, good foreign relations, and healthy economic growth.

Stahl provides many statistical nuggets to support this thesis. Hungary produces several industrial commodities, such as coal and iron ore. Production rates are up 5-8%, and railroad freight is up 16%. He also shows us the growing clout of the middle class. Travel is up 9% yearly, and wine consumption is up 47%.

Additional anecdotal evidence is also provided. In Budapest, "the neighborhood known as the Garden District is now an eclectic mixture of new villas on tree-lined boulevards built by the rising upper middle class." In the middle of the Danube between Pest and Buda, Margaret Island is peppered with summer cottages. And city officials are "most proud of recent accomplishments such as a modern subway and the ice-skating rink in City Park." There are fine restaurants and shops, but Andrassy Boulevard is always crowded.

All in all, it's a nuanced portrait. People want to live here. It is a pleasant place. And economic opportunity abounds. But then Stahl drops the hammer and shatters this idyllic portrait:

"These signs of economic progress are important indicators to those investors who seek opportunity in Hungary. However, at this point it is necessary to admit that a literary device has been used. ... The Hungary which is being described is the Hungary of 1894, not 1994."

An investor in Hungary in 1894 would've lost all of their money if they had not sold ahead of the crisis on the horizon. If you waited too long, you couldn't sell. "In 1914," as Stahl notes, "it was impossible to sell because, upon the outbreak of war in August 1914, the world equity markets were forced to close."

An unknown unknown? Stahl's point is that investing in

"emerging markets" can involve risks that are impossible to know beforehand.

There are plenty of other examples where entire markets delivered basically a zero for public equity investors. China in 1949 or Russia in 1917 quickly come to mind.

All investors must grapple with the concept of "unknown unknowns," and those who venture beyond their home markets face this challenge even more acutely.

Now, if you're investing in the US, Canada, the UK, Australia, or Sweden ... We can agree there isn't (at the time of writing) much country risk in these places that would significantly separate one from another. Most of Western Europe is probably in the same bucket.

But what about Poland? The Warsaw Exchange (in its current form) has existed only since 1991. Is that a step outside the above markets? What about Mexico? What about China?

There are many opportunities to invest in great companies around the world, but how should we approach them?

Thomas Phelps on Getting Away from It All

In his *100 to 1 in the Stock Market,* Phelps wrote about investing abroad. He has a great line in a chapter titled "Getting Away from It All":

> "For most people, investing abroad amounts to fleeing from hazards they can see to hazards they cannot see."

Investors tend to want to invest abroad because they dislike what they see at home. For example, Phelps writes about "sophisticated" American investors investing in Argentina and France to escape the perils of the New Deal and what they expected to be a significant dollar devaluation.

Phelps points out that he doubts they made much money on their foreign adventures. They certainly would have made a lot more by buying bargains at home. "Distance lends enchantment," Phelps writes.

He also remembers how, in 1942, the UK government "sequestered" (a fancy word for "stole") American securities owned by UK citizens to help pay for the war.

Reflecting on the misadventures of investors wandering from their home markets, Phelps comes up with two conclusions:

1. Never invest abroad to escape perils at home *unless you are prepared to go with your money.*

2. Otherwise, invest abroad only when the foreign opportunity seems better by a wide margin than anything you can find at home. That "wide margin" is to cover the difference between what you know about conditions in your native country and the most you can hope to know about a country you have perhaps visited occasionally and studied intermittently from afar.

These seem like sensible conclusions to me.

I am a US-based investor with nine of the 12 stocks I hold not listed in the US. All those nine are in markets I view as being no riskier than the US (Canada, Sweden, the UK, etc.). I have been investing globally since 2004. I wrote a book about some of my travels up to 2012, *World Right Side Up: Investing Across Six Continents.* (Antarctica being the missing continent). When I was younger, I had many misadventures in Mongolia, Greece, Argentina, Colombia, and other places. I got fantastic training and an excellent education in what not to do.

It's Still Worth Exploring Other Markets

So, I'm not against exploring other markets. Neither is Phelps.

In his book, he spends several pages on why Australia should be a source of attractive investments. Keep in mind, he was writing in 1972. To that point, Australia had been a significant market, with the Australian exchange up 60 times in the prior 75 years and more than twice the size of the Dow. All those natural resources were just getting discovered, you know. Phelps mentions the story of Lang Hancock, who made a mountain of money on iron ore royalties. You can almost hear the gears turning in Phelps's head as he ponders the 100-bagger potential of investing in royalties.

Anyway, I wouldn't discourage you from exploring markets outside your home market. However, I would discourage you from relying on the kind of macro chit-chat Stahl pointed to in his Budapest example. People don't know what they are talking about, not because they are not intelligent or well-intentioned, but because what they're trying to know is impossible.

Lastly, I would encourage you to adopt Phelps's two points of advice, especially #2, and consider possible unknowns when investing abroad.

Art Collecting and Investing

Another clue on how to run a portfolio comes to us from the art world.

Sosnoff, who we've checked in with more than a few times on our journey, uses his experience collecting art to illustrate ideas about investing in stocks. The two pursuits share more similarities than one might suspect. Both activities reward patience and a strong stomach. (And, let's face it, luck helps.) Both markets have histories full of seemingly improbable and extreme outcomes, mind-boggling wealth creation and, unfortunately, destruction. Each is humbling to a painful degree.

Consider one of the more unforgettable anecdotes in Sosnoff's book *Train to Outslug the Market.* In 1982, graffiti artist Jean-Michel Basquiat left the streets of New York to hole up in a basement on West Broadway and paint.

Sosnoff got a call from Mary Boone, a trusted art dealer: "You better buy a couple. They're $2,500 apiece." Of course, he declined to invest, instead focusing on some new trendier art from Germany.

"Well," Sosnoff wrote, "nearly 40 years later, one of these Basquiat [paintings] sold at auction for $100 million. Sooo … I could've bought half a dozen Basquiats and made half a billion."

Two thoughts immediately come to mind: one, you can achieve some remarkable results from benign neglect — simply letting a good asset sit for a long time. And two, I doubt anybody holds on to a Basquiat that long if they are getting price quotes put to them every day. The parallels with investing in stocks seem apparent.

I dream of what my portfolio might look like ten years from now. I suspect I may have a couple of giant winners that become outsized chunks of the portfolio. Maybe not a Basquiat, but one can aim high. The biggest challenge will be holding on. Benign neglect sounds easy. In practice, it isn't. There is no escaping the ups and downs. Equanimity is key.

Art and collectible indexes have generally shown returns of about 6% over the last century. That hides stomach-churning volatility, the inevitable roller-coaster rides, and the exponential returns of holding big winners. (It also hides the zeros.)

The same is true with stock indexes. Most stocks are losers, but the returns come from the big winners. Can we put ourselves in a situation to get those big fish? The answer is yes. An easier way of tackling the problem is to invert the question. Let's think about the businesses we'd want to avoid that have no chance or very little chance of creating those kinds of special returns.

A partial list:

- Businesses that aren't growing much
- Businesses that generate poor or mediocre returns on capital
- Businesses that heavily rely on debt
- Businesses that lack ample opportunities to reinvest
- Businesses without strong competitive advantages or moats
- Businesses run by shareholder-unfriendly management teams

Believe it or not, this short list eliminates most businesses. By rejecting most businesses, you can whittle down to a central idea that your portfolio expresses. In fact, what that means is an interesting question to explore.

What Is the Central Idea Behind Your Portfolio?

Sosnoff criticizes what he calls the "pie chart" schemata so often used by investment advisors, where every position is neatly sliced, labeled, and presented in a pie chart. "Intricate chop-chop of client portfolios raises the question," he wrote, "like what is the central idea therein?"

Skin in the game is the central idea expressed in my portfolio. I invest with talented people who have skin in the game. In other words, I invest in businesses where management and/or the board owns a significant amount of stock. Regarding your own portfolio, consider what essential idea your collective holdings express. Once I've checked the skin-in-the-game box, I look for a trio of other attributes, which we've discussed already:

- Earning consistently high returns on capital
- The ability to reinvest and continue to earn those high returns
- A strong balance sheet (I avoid excessive financial leverage).

Those are the essentials. Everything else is a detail.

A Good Filter For Finding Winners – Family Ownership

Remember Sosnoff's line, "entrepreneurial instinct equates with sizable equity ownership?"

I've made this idea a key filter in my investment philosophy. The first thing I do when I look at a business is pull up the proxy. If there are no significant shareholders among the executives and directors, it's an easy pass. I go on to the next name.

Does this mean I'll miss out on great investments run by hired hands with little skin in the game? Of course. A good investment filter makes the investable universe manageable and is essential for managing your time and attention. Filters, by design, exclude. You have to be comfortable knowing that many good ideas will slip through your nets.

A good filter should focus on identifying winners. You want to fish in good waters. Stocks with higher levels of insider ownership tend to outperform their peers, as backed up by various studies. In short, there's good fishing in these pools.

There are many kinds of owners. When you delve into this subject, you discover a great deal of nuance in the whole thing. Over the years, I've developed a list of sub-filters and rules. (For example, never buy anything sold by private equity.) Good ideas always slip by, but my rules have kept me out of trouble. One type of ownership that has fascinated me especially is family ownership. My interest in family businesses led me to work with the Bonner family office in 2016. I've known the Bonners since publishing my newsletter in 2004. Bill Bonner is a partner in Woodlock House Family Capital. And the Bonner family is a major investor in the fund.

Family ownership is naturally suited to making decisions with the long term in mind. If anybody can resist the siren song of short-termism, it would be a family. A good body of academic research indicates that this is indeed the case. My experience working with the Bonners affirms what I have read. They have been ideal partners and investors.

As for that academic research, I came across a piece by the *Harvard Business Review* (HBR), which includes this long-term wisdom:

> "Rather than being obsessed with hitting quarterly earnings targets, as public companies are, family businesses tend to think in terms of generations, which allows them to take actions that put them in [a] better position to endure the tough times."

And here is a specific example of a quantifiable action that allows for that survival:

> "Debt is a great way to fund growth and goose return on equity, but it also puts the company at risk during the inevitable downturns in the economy. Family businesses last longer because they are able to pay the price that longevity requires."

Family businesses tend to use less leverage than their peers. Public companies with family ownership often display the same traits as privately owned family companies. My portfolio includes several family-owned businesses. Indeed, they're great examples of what good family ownership can bring, and how they align with HBR's research.

I've also been reading through bits of the *HBR's Family Business Handbook: How to Build and Sustain a Successful, Enduring Enterprise.* The second chapter is titled "The Power of Family Ownership."

The authors note that the classic corporate pyramid in a typical public company has the CEO at the top, followed by managers and employees below. But in family business ideas, an additional inverted, hidden pyramid rests on top of the classic one:

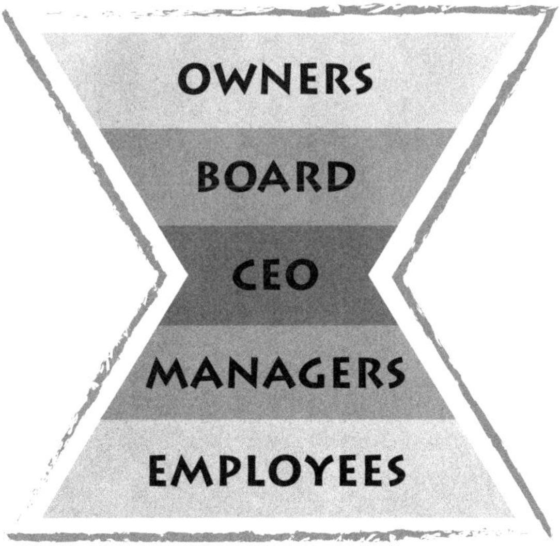

The idea of owners at the top of a pyramid doesn't usually occur in widely held, publicly traded companies because those owners are so diffuse, they turn over frequently, and they have little influence beyond the buying and selling of shares. Such owners are more likely to be a nuisance to management than to feel responsible toward anything.

I like the idea of the inverted pyramid. It's a way to think about your portfolio companies. Where does the power lie? Is it with the CEO? The board? The owners? Are you okay with the answers to these questions?

Thinking through these issues is essential for long-term business investors. Confidence in the people at the helm will make enduring corrections much more manageable.

Troubled times often present opportunities for entrepreneurs. And you know what Sosnoff says about entrepreneurial instinct.

Making Sense of Insider Buys/Sells

One question arises, primarily when investing alongside owners. How do we interpret insider buying and selling?

It may seem obvious, but insider buying and selling research is murky. Professor Aswath Damodaran calls insider buying "a noisy signal" because about four in 10 stocks where insiders are buying don't work out well. On average, the excess returns earned are not substantial.

Likewise, insider selling generally predicts no worse returns, on average. But not always.

For example, a study by James Scott and Peter Xu (2004) found that only large sales predicted negative returns. Small sales, as a percentage of overall insider holdings, "not only did not predict poor performance but were correlated with significantly positive abnormal returns." Go figure.

When interpreting insider buys and sells, I always think of George Muzea. He wrote *The Vital Few vs. The Trivial Many,* which I read when it was published in 2003. It has stayed with me ever since.

Muzea's premise is simple. He says it's natural for an insider to buy when a stock is down, and it's also expected that they will take money off the table when a stock has had a great run. However, we shouldn't give much weight to those signals.

Look for divergence. Pay special attention to insiders buying *after* a stock has already made a big move. On the other hand, look for insiders who are selling *after* a stock has already been chopped up.

Here are a few more suggestions:

1. Look for many insider purchases or sales. If the chairman, CEO, and CFO are all buying, that seems worth paying attention to.
2. Focus on key people. Although there is always some selling, I focus on central roles, such as the CEO and CFO.
3. Amounts matter. I'd ignore token buys or small sales from more extensive holdings.
4. The signal is more potent for small caps. Some research suggests that insider signaling is ineffective for large-cap companies. It also makes sense. It's easier for an insider to know what's happening in a smaller company than for an insider to know what's going on at, for example, GE.

Insider buying and selling can be a valuable tool for identifying investment ideas. However, the signal value of insider transactions seems noisy and is not as simple as it may seem. As a long-term owner of businesses, it's probably not worth focusing on.

What Have You Done For Me This Morning?

I suspect a short time horizon is one reason why mutual funds often own so many stocks. Since mutual funds are frequently priced, they are frequently evaluated, and few managers want to risk being out of step for long. There is pressure for short-term performance. We get statements monthly, or sometimes quarterly. Investors study those statements to get some sense of how they're doing.

Clients asking their fund managers "What have you done for me this morning?" is an old problem. It is hard to fix without the proper setup and good partners. Individual investors have no such pressures — to their great advantage.

I aim to own my stocks forever. Not literally forever, but I abide by Buffett's dictum: "If you aren't thinking about owning a stock for ten years, don't even think about owning it for ten minutes." It's one of the best filters I use.

Academic finance tends to think differently. Block, who we introduced in the previous chapter, mentions Harry Markowitz and his idea of an "efficient portfolio" that maximizes the risk-return combination. Markowitz may be a dated example, but Block makes the excellent point that any idea of "efficiency" implies a lot of trading:

> "It is not hard to imagine the designing and construction of an 'efficient portfolio' at a given point in time. Yet, the moment that either prices or expectations change, one no longer has a perfect portfolio. Purchases and sales would have to be made continuously. ... The manager would find that its time horizon had collapsed to virtually zero and that its turnover was nearly infinite."

You could rebalance every quarter or year, but such strategies hold no appeal to me. I have nightmares about the taxes. But aside from that, I disagree with Block's view that an "efficient portfolio" is "not hard to imagine." The assumption is that you can accurately measure risk and reliably estimate potential return. I don't think so. I find the idea of an optimized portfolio to be pure fantasy. Real life is messy.

Also, mathematically driven models can recommend you do seemingly nutty things. Block notes that there is no constraint inherent in Markowitz's efficient portfolio. So, for example, it might dictate that you put 90% in one stock and 10% in the Treasury Bills. This reminds me of the popular Kelly Criterion about bet sizing. It, too, can recommend dangerously large bets depending on the inputs. Even people who love the Kelly Criterion often recommend taking positions that are half, or one-quarter the size of what the model says.

I don't worry about whether my portfolio is "optimized" at any given moment. And I dislike the idea you sometimes hear that "if you hold a stock at today's price, it's like buying it." I like to let my portfolio grow like an unruly garden.

Cutting Flowers, Watering Weeds

Contrary to my unruly garden, the mantra of diversification has investors cut back on winners and add to losers, a process Peter Lynch described as "pulling out the flowers and watering the weeds."

The ability to let winners run and become a large part of one's portfolio is a vital ingredient to long-term outperformance. I expect (hope!) at least one of the stocks I own to perform so well that it becomes a massive position over time. It would be tragic to cut that wonderful process short by trimming back a winner regularly. Certainly, our lady from Nantucket never did that. Nor did Sam Walton.

One thing that emerges from Block's essay is how various "portfolio elements are deeply intertwined." He says, "It seems impossible to discuss any single element without considering the inter-relationship with several of the other elements." For example, diversification, time horizon, and risk all interact with one another.

Unfortunately, there are no easy recipes for creating (and managing) a portfolio. However, we've identified a rough set of guidelines to consider. Portfolio management, like a favorite recipe, must be adjusted to suit one's personal taste.

TOP TAKEAWAYS

1. *Portfolio management is an under-appreciated skill that can turn a good investor into a mediocre one, and vice versa.*

2. *Start positions with room to buy more.*

3. *The most risky position in your portfolio is the newest one.*

4. *Only replace when something is way better. Don't talk yourself into taking marginal upgrades.*

5. *Only part with cash when you have something compelling to do with it.*

6. *Invest abroad only when the opportunity is significantly better than what's available at home.*

7. *Thinking exercise: what is the central idea expressed in your portfolio?*

8. *Family ownership is a good filter for finding outperformers.*

9. *Interpreting insider buying and selling: Look for divergence — an insider buys after a big move and sells after a stock has fallen.*

10. *Let winners run.*

CHAPTER 12

Are You a Good Investor?

I NEVER GOT her name, the lady from Nantucket. But her odyssey teaches investors all they need to know about being a good (or even a great) investor. Ultimately, it's straightforward. Buy a high-quality business run by reasonably trustworthy people, and hold onto it for a long time. Simple, but not easy.

Now in this book, I've tried to give you ways to understand the ingredients and how to use them in real life.

What is a high-quality business? We looked at return on invested capital. We looked at reinvestment. We looked at competitive advantages. We ran through a number of examples, everything from commercial insurance brokers to Swedish serial acquirers, from a Polish grocery store to a trucking company.

What about the people? We've looked at the value of owner-operators, of having skin in the game. We've considered corporate culture and the evaluation methods for it.

Finally, you have to hold on for a long time. We looked at what you can expect when you do so. There are wild ups and downs and even years where stocks go nowhere amidst a multi-bagger run. We considered various ways to help extend the time you hold onto stocks, from the coffee can to creating tables of specific performance metrics. Anything to take your focus away from the movements of stock prices and instead plant it firmly on the business.

A profusion of details surround all of these things. But in the end, it's simple. Anything that takes you away from thinking about your stocks in terms of decades is a distraction. If you keep to this as your North Star, a lot of unnecessary baggage will naturally slip away.

If you're committed to owning a business, you'll find a whole range of things you won't care about much anymore. You won't particularly care if there is a recession coming. Over the course of owning your business, you will likely experience several recessions. You won't particularly care about which political party is in control (as long as democracy is in place) or what interest rates will do. You'll likely own your business under a variety of administrations, through periods where interest rates are rising, and through periods where they're falling.

Not only does unnecessary baggage slip away, but good habits naturally arise. You will be much more careful about what you buy in the first place. Buying and selling stocks should be approached with the same level of care as entering into a marriage.

Your attention will also naturally turn toward things that matter in the long term. You will be more interested in cash flows and return on capital, the underlying engine that generates returns in your business over the course of a decade or more. You won't care much about what next quarter will look like or how it will compare to the quarter a year ago. Ten years is 40 quarters worth of results, which puts things in proper perspective.

Finally, there is a benefit to the approach advocated for in this book that often goes underappreciated. That has to do with the quality of your life. Not focused on the day-to-day media circus, you will find more time for reflection on broader, more substantive issues. Less time reading the latest take on social media means more time for books. Less time in front of your computer watching stock prices means more time for contemplative walks or time with friends.

Hopefully, you will have taken yourself outside of the rat race of worrying about your portfolio's returns. You may find great pleasure in watching your companies grow over the years, if you've chosen well. With luck, you may see amazing things happen. For example, in years to come, your company could report profits that exceed the total sales when you bought it. As an illustrative example (and certainly not typical): When I first bought Constellation

Software, it reported C$3.4 billion in sales in 2019. In 2024, it reported gross profits of C$3.4 billion. That's what compounding can do in only five years. Think what can happen over a decade or longer. Study the results of winning businesses over the long term and get a feel for what can be achieved.

As for your returns, you may start to measure them not in terms of percentages, but in how far the stock price is above your cost, such as 4x or 10x (or perhaps even 100x).

You should feel a certain calm that comes from knowing what you own and being comfortable not touching your account. Recall what Dean Williams told us in his speech "Trying Too Hard"—most of the effort and activity that people put into investing does not translate into better returns. Williams makes a compelling case for an investing life without forecasts, a simple investment plan, and humility about what's possible to know.

Martin Sosnoff echoed this simplicity with his minimalist approach. Remember Sosnoff's Law, that the return you earn on an investment varies inversely with the thickness of the research file. Again, it's hard to over-emphasize the power of a simple compelling investment idea.

That lady from Nantucket couldn't have had a simpler plan. She stuck with Warren, through thick and thin, through booms and busts. She was as kind and gentle a soul as you'd ever meet. Money didn't mess her up, or so it seemed. She earned it, over time. You may not get as rich as she did. But I'm confident you'll be rich enough and decadent in ways not counted in dollars.

How Do You Evaluate A Money Manager?

Sizing up a money manager is tricky. Track records can be deceiving and challenging to parse. What sort of risks did the manager take in generating returns? What kind of luck factor was involved? Or, put another way, how repeatable does it seem? How can you benchmark their performance?

One of the simplest ways to evaluate managers is to see if they did what they said they would do. In my case, I've made a big deal out of investing with management teams that have skin in the game. I always talk about it in my letters and discussions with my investors. If I go off and buy a company where the insiders own 1% of the shares, you might reasonably ask what is going on regardless of whether that particular position worked out.

There can be gray areas. For example, while there isn't a lot of skin in the game percentage-wise, the insiders have much of their net worth at stake, and the incentives are well-aligned due to a novel compensation plan. (I have made no such exception so far; I'm using this as an example to make a point.)

You may say, "Okay, that makes sense," and agree. But if I repeatedly make excuses for names in a portfolio that doesn't seem to be what I promised to create, that would be a red flag and a reason to withdraw, regardless of how I have performed.

Integrity is far more critical than single-year, three-year, or five-year performance figures. And this is a lesson learned from spending a long time in the game. Plenty of investors flame out after good performance streaks, for various reasons. One reason is that the investor lacked a good process to begin with, or had one but failed to stick to it (especially difficult when enduring a soft patch in performance).

Long-term success in this business stems from identifying a niche area of expertise and sticking to it. Your circle of preference. This doesn't mean you don't evolve and change. You do. You should also evolve and change as you gain new experiences. But you shouldn't let the market winds blow you off course, changing your strategy to fit whatever is hot.

There are always exceptions, like talented and bold people who frequently change their stripes, turn over their portfolio every year, and continue to deliver significant returns. It's one of the glorious things about investing — there are so many ways to do it.

My interest in investing has always been more focused on what's straightforward and repeatable. It has a very good chance of working over the long haul, without doing anything risky where

I could lose everything (or nearly everything). That's why I started my book *100 Baggers* with tales of ordinary people making a lot of money doing something simple: buying good businesses and holding on to them.

Some people mock that insight as obvious, unworthy of book-length treatment, or somehow insufficient. It's as if the people who nabbed those 100-baggers were merely lucky. I couldn't disagree more. The power of holding on is the most critical lesson for almost everyone.

In the parlance of our times, the ability to hold on is a superpower. It's much more complicated than it sounds, as anyone who invests for any time will find out. Sitting through 30% and 50% drawdowns is excruciating. Hanging on when people tell you that what you own is no good — and when they keep telling you to buy a different shiny new toy — is even more challenging.

How to Get Rich? Not How You Expect

Let's conclude with a different perspective on success in the markets, one that extends beyond your return. For this discussion, we're bringing in Felix Dennis.

Felix Dennis was one of our most colorful entrepreneurs. He died from throat cancer on June 22, 2014, at the age of 67. If you've never read his book, *How to Get Rich,* you're missing out on the best book of its kind. But more on that in a bit.

Felix Dennis was one of the wealthiest self-made men in the United Kingdom. He started with nothing. No capital and no college education. Dennis made his money publishing hobbyist and lifestyle magazines, beginning with *Kung-Fu Monthly* in 1974. He then added many more titles, including *Maxim* and *The Week.*

In the early years, he spent a lot of money on booze, women, and drugs, but he eventually cleaned up his personal life. He became fond of planting trees and created a charity that planted its two millionth tree in March 2022. He was also fond of poetry and wrote his first poem in 2001. Since then, he's written several well-regarded books of poetry.

I've read numerous obituaries about the man that relate various amusing anecdotes. David Cherry, who used to work for Dennis, wrote: "When NYC banned smoking in workplaces in the late 1990s, Felix's response was simply, 'Let me know what the fine is.'"

In an interview with *The Guardian* in 2010, Dennis said that the most critical lesson life had taught him was this: "Fear nothing — failing that, fake it!" Asked how he would like to be remembered, he said, "Truly, I could not care less."

Just how rich was Felix Dennis? He said he didn't know. He owned many businesses, houses, cars, thousands of acres of land, bronze statues, art on the walls, and libraries stuffed with first editions. "Oh, and thousands of bottles of fine wine in the cellars," he said. "Never forget the wine."

Who knows what all that stuff was worth? He quoted J. Paul Getty, who once said, "If you can actually count your money, then you are not really a rich man." Forced to guess, Dennis put his fortune somewhere between $400 million and $900 million. "I honestly cannot fix a number any closer than that."

You can count on a refreshingly honest opinion delivered with panache from Dennis. That brings us to *How to Get Rich,* a little gem of a book.

For one thing, unlike a lot of such books, Dennis wrote it himself. There is no co-author or ghostwriter. It's a good thing, too, because Dennis was a good writer. Second, he got rich *before* he wrote the book.

More importantly, the tone of his book is entirely different from anything in the genre because Dennis wrote extensively about the personal costs of getting rich. He tells you how hard it is. He points out how it changes your relationships with people. He never lets you forget how much time it will take out of your days and nights.

There are plenty of places in the book where he — well, I won't say he discourages you per se, but he forces you to be honest with yourself about what you value. Because in the quest to get rich, getting rich must be at the top of the list.

The most important part of the book is found in a chapter called “A Recap for Idlers.” The key point is that the richest are those with the most time. “If you are young,” Dennis writes, “you are infinitely richer than I can ever be again.”

So think carefully about whether you want to spend that time getting rich, he advises. No matter how wealthy you get, you cannot reclaim the lost time. These pages of the book are the most poignant and memorable. For example:

> “I have been inferior and I am now wealthy. I am an optimist by nature. And I can write poetry and create the forest I am busy planting. Am I happy? No. Or, at least, only occasionally, when I am walking in the woods alone, or deeply ensconced in composing a difficult piece of verse, or sitting quietly with old friends over a bottle of wine. Or feeding a stray cat. ... I could do all those things without wealth.”

No matter how you invest or your track record, remember that the things that matter most to you likely have little to do with either. Enjoy the journey.

One Last Thing...

The cover of this book is from a painting by another Felix, Félix Ziem. As we were putting the finishing touches on the book, my editor Eddie Palmgren found an article titled “How to Get Rich as an Artist: The Case of Félix Ziem.”

Per the article, Ziem was a tailor’s son who made financial success as a painter. His annual salary was top-six percent in France and about 100 times that a family of small farmers. He owned annuities, bonds, and shares in the 1850s. Also, “he became the first artist whose works entered the Louvre Museum during his lifetime.”

The article doesn't say whether Ziem was happy. But as Felix Dennis taught us, financial success doesn't come for free. Ziem's "rigorous accounting reflected more a businessperson's attitude toward the art market than a bohemian one. Paul Durand-Ruel confirmed this when he wrote, 'Ziem has always had a flaw: he loved money too much. It brings about the artist's ruin.'"

What about us as investors? How can we refrain from loving money too much? If you find yourself obsessing over your portfolio's results and neglecting other areas of your life, you may love the money too much. But there is more to it than this.

I believe that investing is something you will have a better chance of success with if you love the *process.* That is, if you enjoy learning about companies and how they work:

- You are fascinated by the successes (and failures) and want to know more about how they happened.
- You get excited when you find an opportunity that fits what you're looking for.
- You get a kick out of watching these companies grow in your portfolio, seeing their sales and profits rise over the years, and celebrating milestones along the way.

Each company becomes its own mini-drama, a story more riveting than that of any sports team or TV series. As you own these companies for years, your knowledge about them (and the ecosystem in which they operate) will deepen. You'll understand their strengths and weaknesses better. You'll be able to discern what really matters and what's noise.

These are things that make up the art of investing. You may or may not make a lot of money as an investor. But starting merely out of a desire to make a lot of money likely won't sustain you for the long investor's odyssey.

That journey is beset with many tests and challenges. Gratification is often delayed. In fact, it may never come. Your returns are back-end loaded; it could take years before you see big, life-changing successes.

Those who thrive are the ones who bind themselves to the mast of their craft, and resist the Siren song of quick riches. Play the long game, and you will make it home.

AFTERWORD

About Chris Mayer

FOR THOSE WHO DON'T know me or want to learn more, here is a brief interlude on my unconventional path to where I am — I hope you will find it instructive.

I grew up in a financially secure family. My mother was a banker. My father worked at the insurance company GEICO for more than three decades. I heard stories of the young Warren Buffett visiting Lorimer Davidson, the CEO at what would become GEICO, one Saturday morning in 1951. When I wanted to learn more about investing and the stock market, particularly after the 1987 crash, which intrigued me and deepened the mystery of people winning and losing large sums of money, Warren Buffett was the obvious choice to study. My parents had a subscription to *Fortune Magazine,* and as a teenager, I read stories about Buffett and investing. His teacher was Benjamin Graham, and I sought out Graham's magisterial book, *Security Analysis.*

This large, dense book was a magical tome to me. I distinctly remember talking about it at a family dinner and bringing out a copy I purchased to show off this marvelous brick of a book by Warren Buffett's teacher. Here lie the secrets of how to make a lot of money in the stock market. I couldn't make heads or tails of it then, but I knew I wanted to understand it. I wanted to learn. I needed a lot of education first, particularly in accounting. I would go on to study finance in college. And eventually, that magical book started to make sense.

My path was set at an early age, although I perhaps didn't appreciate it then. I explored other paths in my twenties and early thirties. I read and studied books on all kinds of methods: reading charts, special situations, options, etc. The notion of stocks representing a share of a business never left me, though. Ultimately, that is where I settled in.

I also took a circuitous path to money management. After college, I went into commercial banking. It was a good place to learn a lot about different businesses. I got good training on balance sheets and the importance of creditworthiness. All of this experience resonated with me after reading Graham's book.

I loved investing and gobbled up all kinds of books about it. The 1990s were still the era of the star fund manager. I read books by Peter Lynch, Robert Wanger, John Neff, and other notable investors, and explored various investing styles. It took me a long time before investing became a cohesive set of principles.

In 2004, I started my financial newsletter, which focused on investing. I wrote about investing ideas and tracked a model portfolio. Meant to be a night and weekend project, I had no idea where it would lead.

But the newsletter quickly built a following. After six months, I had about 150 paying subscribers. This was before Substack, X (formerly Twitter), and all the other online avenues available today, so it was harder to get noticed. My wife and I stuffed envelopes and mailed issues to the subscribers every month. Soon, I made a deal with a publisher in Baltimore called Agora, which is mainly owned by the Bonner family. I dropped my banking job and wrote my letter full-time.

I traveled worldwide and met all kinds of people while writing that letter. It was a life-changing endeavor. At one point, I had over 40,000 subscribers. I wrote missives from Bangkok to Buenos Aires, Mongolia to Peru. I wrote about all kinds of businesses in all kinds of markets. What an education and what an adventure.

One central turning point came when I read Chuck Akre's 2011 speech, "An Investor's Odyssey: The Search for Outstanding Investments." Akre is another great investor who has shaped my thinking more than anyone besides Buffett and Munger. In this speech, Akre mentioned a book called *100 to 1 in the Stock Market,* by Thomas Phelps, which he said had a significant influence on him. I had never heard of it, and I thought I had read every investing book there was.

I hunted down a copy. Phelps studies the stocks that returned at least 100 to 1, turning a $10,000 investment into $1,000,000. A 100-bagger. It's an excellent book, and I loved it. I quoted from it often. One day, a subscriber said I should update it — light bulb. Great idea.

The outcome of that effort was my book, *100 Baggers,* which was published in 2015 and significantly influenced my approach to investing. Most of this book is the distilled wisdom from that raw study (along with my experiences applying it). Like Phelps, I looked at all the stocks that had returned at least 100 to 1. My findings echoed Phelps and were eye-opening.

In 2016, I started working with the Bonner family office. My newsletter's model portfolio had a strong track record, and I was eager to help invest the family's money. Families can provide a stellar home for good investing because they can take the long view and be patient. I have gotten to know the Bonners over the years, and they are undoubtedly patient and play the long game. I enjoyed helping them, and this relationship led to the next chapter of my story.

Bill Bonner (the family patriarch) and I founded Woodlock House Family Capital in late 2018, though the idea had been bubbling for over three years. (The fund's start date was January 2, 2019, the first business day of the New Year).

The firm's name comes from the Bonner family's property, Woodlock House, in Portlaw, Ireland. The main house dates back to 1864. It was a family home, a convent, and a nursing home. Today, it houses several publishing businesses owned by the Bonner family. The Woodlock House Family Capital logo depicts the skylight in the grand foyer.

I visited in the summer of 2018. Since Bill and I sealed the deal in Ireland, we thought the house would be a good name for the firm. The house itself exudes a classic staying power, rich in history yet adapting to the changing times.

We added "family" because the capital initially invested in starting the firm and investing in the fund was family money. There is a lot of skin in the game. The firm's purpose was to solve a problem: How can we invest our family wealth without turning it over to Wall Street and people without skin in the game?

The word "family" reflects a basic orientation. Successful families tend to think of the next generation. They tend to be patient. They tend to use less debt. You can see all this in the behavior of publicly traded firms controlled by families. (These firms also tend to outperform their peers.)

These timeless principles yield long-term performance. I trust in experience over theory and value the tested over the unproven. Old-fashioned effort, careful study, and a healthy appreciation of uncertainty reap rewards. So here I am today, managing the portfolio at Woodlock House, where I'm putting into practice what I learned from Akre, Phelps, and my study of 100-baggers.

— *Chris Mayer, January 2026*

APPENDIX: RETURN ON INVESTED CAPITAL CALCULATION

The standard formula for return on invested capital:

$$\text{Return on Invested Capital (ROIC)} = \frac{\text{Net Operating Profit After Tax (NOPAT)}}{\text{Invested Capital (IC)}}$$

Where *NOPAT* is:
- EBITA - cash taxes

And where *invested capital* is:
- Net working capital + Net property, plant, & equipment + Acquired intangibles + Goodwill + Preferred stock + Other Assets

And *Net working capital* is:
- Current assets - non-interest bearing liabilities

Or, for a rough shortcut, invested capital equals net working capital + non-current assets + preferred stock.

There are other ways to calculate invested capital. It can get complicated, depending on the business and the number of adjustments you make.

For example, if you really want to get into the weeds on calculating ROIC, seek out "Return on Invested Capital: How to Calculate ROIC and Handle Common Issues," by Michael Mauboussin and Dan Callahan, available for free online.

There are other return metrics you could consider, such as return on equity and return on capital employed. They all measure different things and have different strengths and weaknesses.

Don't worry too much about the specific calculations. For a truly excellent business, the economics will be obvious and compelling. If you are spending a lot of time with spreadsheets and decimal points, you're probably not dealing with a great business.

The main idea here is to get you to think about something beyond the usual earnings and growth rates that everyone talks about, and instead consider how much capital a business requires to generate those earnings and growth rates.

ACKNOWLEDGEMENTS

I would like to thank Eddie Palmgren, who served as editor on this project. His help was invaluable and the book is much improved thanks to his efforts.

Thanks to Myles Thompson, my publisher at Partners Media, for his many good suggestions and wise guidance throughout the process.

Thanks to Chuck Akre for allowing me to reprint a part of his speech for the foreword.

And thanks to Yvonne Münzberg for a great-looking cover.

VISUALS

BIBLIOGRAPHY

Introduction

Williams, Dean. "Trying Too Hard." Keynote speech at the Financial Analysts Federation Seminar, Rockford College, Rockford, IL, August 9, 1981.

Mayer, Christopher W. *How Do You Know?: A Guide to Clear Thinking About Wall Street, Investing & Life*. USA: Bonner & Partners, 2018.

Armstrong, J. Scott. "Unintelligible Management Research and Academic Prestige." Interfaces 10, no. 2 (April 1980): 80–86. https://ssrn.com/abstract=676112.

Sosnoff, Martin T. *Humble on Wall Street*. New York: Arlington House Publishers, 1975.

Sosnoff, Martin. *Silent Investor, Silent Loser*. New York: Richardson & Steirman, 1986.

Sosnoff, Martin. *Master Class for Investors: Stand Alone to Win Big*. New York: Atalanta Press, 2015.

Homer. *The Odyssey*. Translated by Robert Fagles. New York: Viking, 1996. Original work published ca. 8th century BCE.

Chapter 1

Jackson, Peter, dir. *The Lord of the Rings: The Fellowship of the Ring*. Featuring Elijah Wood, Ian McKellen, and Viggo Mortensen. New Line Cinema, 2001. 178 min.

LRT Capital Management: November 2021 Investor Update.

Bilello, Charlie (@charliebilello). X profile. https://x.com/charliebilello.

Bessembinder, Hendrik. "Extreme Stock Market Performers, Part I: Expect Some Drawdowns." SSRN Scholarly Paper. Rochester, NY: Social Science Research Network, July 21, 2020. https://papers.ssrn.com/sol3/papers.cfm?abstract_id=3657604.

Gavin Baker, "Interview with Gavin Baker," Graham & Doddsville, no. 43 (Fall 2021): 25, https://business.columbia.edu/sites/default/files-efs/imce-uploads/Graham%20%26%20Doddsville_Issue%2043_vF.pdf.

Oldfield, Richard. *Simple but Not Easy: A Guide to the World of Practical Investing*. London: Harriman House, 2007.

Mayer, Christopher W. *100 Baggers: Stocks that Return 100-to-1 and How to Find Them.* Laissez Faire Books, 2015.

Catalyst Insights. "Lessons from Peter Lynch: Invest in What You Know." Accessed December 17, 2025. https://catalyst-insights.com/lessons-from-peter-lynch-invest-in-what-you-know/.

"What happened and why?" The Journal of Portfolio Management 6, no. 1 (Fall 1979): 4–13. https://www.pm-research.com/content/iijpormgmt/6/1.

Bernstein, Peter L. *Against the Gods: The Remarkable Story of Risk.* New York: John Wiley & Sons, 1996.

Capital Ideas: The Improbable Origins of Modern Wall Street. New York: Free Press, 1992.

Buffett, Warren, and Charlie Munger. "1997 Annual Shareholder Meeting." Berkshire Hathaway. Omaha, NE, May 5, 1997.

Chapter 2

Bilello, Charlie. "The Week in Charts (4/14/25)." Charlie Bilello's Blog, April 14, 2025. https://bilello.blog/2025/the-week-in-charts-4-14-25.

Zeikel, Arthur. "After 50 years, nothing new, nor likely." The Journal of Portfolio Management 6, no. 1 (Fall 1979): 26–35. https://doi.org/10.3905/jpm.1979.408706.

Watts, Alan. Tao: *The Watercourse Way.* New York: Pantheon Books, 1975.

Buffett, Warren E. "Chairman's Letter - 1997." Berkshire Hathaway Inc. March 14, 1998. https://www.berkshirehathaway.com/letters/1997.html.

Watzlawick, Paul. *The Situation Is Hopeless, but Not Serious: The Pursuit of Unhappiness.* New York: W. W. Norton & Company, 1983.

Lowenstein, Louis. *What's Wrong with Wall Street: Short-Term Gain and the Corporate Efficiency Myth.* New York: Addison-Wesley, 1988.

Lowenstein, Roger. *Buffett: The Making of an American Capitalist.* New York: Random House, 1995.

Postman, Neil. *Technopoly: The Surrender of Culture to Technology.* New York: Alfred A. Knopf, 1992.

Postman, Neil. *Amusing Ourselves to Death: Public Discourse in the Age of Show Business.* New York: Viking Penguin, 1985.

Postman, Neil, and Steve Powers. *How to Watch TV News.* New York: Penguin Books, 1992.

Phelps, Thomas William. *100 to 1 in the Stock Market: A Distinguished Security Analyst Tells How to Make More of Your Money.* New York: McGraw-Hill, 1972.

"What happened and why?" The Journal of Portfolio Management 6, no. 1 (Fall 1979): 4–13. https://www.pm-research.com/content/iijpormgmt/6/1.

Akre, Chuck. "The Bottom Line of All Investing Is Rate of Return." Akre Capital Management (blog). Accessed December 17, 2025. https://www.akrecapital.com/the-bottom-line-of-all-investing-is-rate-of-return/.

Gracián, Baltasar. *The Art of Worldly Wisdom: A Pocket Oracle.* Translated by Christopher Maurer. New York: Doubleday, 1992. Original work published 1647.

Akre Capital Management. "Why Compounding Is So Difficult." Accessed December 17, 2025. https://www.akrecapital.com/why-compounding-is-so-difficult/.

Kirby, Robert G. "The Coffee Can Portfolio." The Journal of Portfolio Management 11, no. 1 (Fall 1984): 76–80. DOI: 10.3905/jpm.1984.408988

Shell, Adam. "Tread Carefully in a Hot IPO Market." Kiplinger, February 1, 2021. https://www.kiplinger.com/investing/stocks/602118/tread-carefully-in-a-hot-ipo-market.

Bessembinder, Hendrik, Te-Feng Chen, Goeun Choi, and Kuo-Chiang Wei. "Long-Term Shareholder Returns: Evidence from 64,000 Global Stocks." Financial Analysts Journal 79, no. 3 (2023): 33–63. https://dx.doi.org/10.2139/ssrn.3710251

Bender, Ruth, and Inti Landauro. "Vivendi to Sell Remaining Activision Blizzard Stake." The Wall Street Journal, May 22, 2014. https://www.wsj.com/articles/SB10001424052702303749904579577182221768294.

Chapter 3

Buffett, Warren E. "Chairman's Letter - 1992." Berkshire Hathaway Inc. March 1, 1993. https://www.berkshirehathaway.com/letters/1992.html.

Chapter 4

Sosnoff, Martin T. *Humble on Wall Street.* New York: Arlington House Publishers, 1975.

Sosnoff, Martin. *Silent Investor, Silent Loser.* New York: Richardson & Steirman, 1986.

Brown & Brown, Inc. Form 10-K for the Fiscal Year Ended December 31, 2022. Filed February 27, 2023. https://investor.bbrown.com/sec-filings/sec-filing/10-k/0000950170-23-004717.

Old Dominion Freight Line, Inc. Form 10-K for the Fiscal Year Ended December 31, 2022. Filed February 22, 2023. https://ir.odfl.com/sec-filings/all-sec-filings/content/0000950170-23-013010/odfl_2022_annual_report.pdf.

Weber Logistics, Vice President Transportation. "Old Dominion Freight Line, Inc." Interview by Tegus. February 9, 2023.

"Constellation Software: Culture & M&A." Interview with former Portfolio M&A Leader at Constellation Software. In Practise, February 12, 2022. https://inpractise.com/articles/constellation-software-culture-and-manda.

Buffett, Warren E. "Berkshire Hathaway Inc.: An Owner's Manual." Berkshire Hathaway Inc. January 1999. https://www.berkshirehathaway.com/owners.html.

Chapter 5

Leonard, Connor. IMC Presentation to the Value Investing Club at Google, February 2019.

Koller, Tim, Marc Goedhart, and David Wessels. *Valuation: Measuring and Managing the Value of Companies.* 7th ed. McKinsey & Company. Hoboken, NJ: John Wiley & Sons, 2020.

Chapter 6

Leonard, Mark. "Letter to Shareholders." Constellation Software Inc. February 15, 2021. https://www.csisoftware.com/docs/default-source/press-releases/letter-to-shareholders---february-15-2021.pdf.

Constellation Software Inc. "Constellation Software Inc. Announces the Resignation of Mark Leonard and Appointment of Mark Miller as President of Constellation Software." September 25, 2025. https://www.csisoftware.com/category/press-releases/2025/09/25/constellation-software-inc.-announces-the-resignation-of-mark-leonard-and-appointment-of-mark-miller-as-president-of-constellation-software.

Mayer, Christopher W. *100 Baggers: Stocks that Return 100-to-1 and How to Find Them.* Laissez Faire Books, 2015.

Phelps, Thomas William. *100 to 1 in the Stock Market: A Distinguished Security*

Analyst Tells How to Make More of Your Money. New York: McGraw-Hill, 1972.

Eyesan, Dede. "Global Outperformers." Jenga Investment Partners. January 2023. https://jengaip.com/globaloutperformers/.

Bruner, Robert F. *Deals from Hell: M&A Lessons that Rise Above the Ashes.* Hoboken, NJ: John Wiley & Sons, 2005.

Financial Times. "A Very Secretive Success Story." August 23, 2004. https://www.ft.com/content/b721b37a-efa7-11d8-b4ef-00000e2511c8.

Barber, David. "Delivering Shareholder Value." Strategy Speech, Halma plc. 1997. https://www.halma.com/~/media/Files/H/Halma/Corp-V2/documents/david-barber-halma-strategy-speech.pdf.

Reiner, Thomas. "Tech Company Dilution: Finding Ground Truth." Platform Aeronaut. November 10, 2023. https://www.platformaeronaut.com/p/tech-company-dilution-finding-ground.

Halma plc. Annual Report and Accounts 2025. June 2025. https://www.halma.com/~/media/Files/H/Halma/Corp-V2/reports-and-presentations/reports/2025/Halma-ara-2425.pdf.

Chapter 7

Munger, Charles T. *Poor Charlie's Almanack: The Wit and Wisdom of Charles T. Munger.* Edited by Peter D. Kaufman. 3rd ed. Virginia Beach, VA: PCA Publication, 2005.

Forbes. "America's Richest Families." December 3, 2009. https://www.forbes.com/2009/12/03/americas-richest-families-walton-rockefeller-dupont-business-billionaires-families.html.

Sleep, Nick, and Qais Zakaria. *Nomad Investment Partnership Letters: 2001–2014.* London: I.G.Y. Ltd., 2021.

Mayer, Christopher W. *100 Baggers: Stocks that Return 100-to-1 and How to Find Them.* Laissez Faire Books, 2015.

Cooke, Dom. "The Last Human Edge." Colossus. December 2025. https://joincolossus.com/article/henry-ellenbogen-last-human-edge/.

Nathanson, S. Allen. *Bullishly Speaking: The Writings of Master Investor S. Allen Nathanson 1966-1973, 1980.* Edited by David Seidenfeld, 2002.

Chapter 8

Young, Matthew. "Truckers' Valuations Overheating." Morningstar.

April 19, 2018. https://www.morningstar.com/stocks/truckers-valuations-overheating.

Old Dominion Freight Line, Inc. "ODFL Investor Presentation Q4 2019." February 2020.

Scuttleblurb. "[ODFL – Old Dominion Freight Line] Superb Logistics Company." 2017. https://www.scuttleblurb.com/category/odfl-old-dominion/.

Brown, J. Hyatt. "Simpkins Speaker Series: Hyatt Brown." Recorded at Eastern Florida State College, February 2020. Video, 1:04:22. https://www.youtube.com/watch?v=luinAI0NSq8.

Wepler, John. "The M&A Valuation Secret of Insurance Brokerages." Today's ViewPoint (blog). Marshberry, August 16, 2022. https://www.marshberry.com/resource/the-ma-valuation-dirty-little-secret/.

U.S. Department of Justice. "Justice Department Sues to Block Aon's Acquisition of Willis Towers Watson." June 16, 2021. https://www.justice.gov/archives/opa/pr/justice-department-sues-block-aon-s-acquisition-willis-towers-watson.

Chapter 9

"McKinsey on Finance." Number 84, December 2023. https://www.mckinsey.com/capabilities/strategy-and-corporate-finance/our-insights/mckinsey-on-finance/mckinsey-on-finance-number-84.

Mayer, Christopher W. *100 Baggers: Stocks that Return 100-to-1 and How to Find Them.* Laissez Faire Books, 2015.

TenHaken, Vicky. *Lessons from Century Club Companies: Managing for Long-Term Success.* Holland, MI: Hope College, 2016.

Sagan, Carl. *The Varieties of Scientific Experience: A Personal View of the Search for God.* Edited by Ann Druyan. New York: Penguin Press, 2006.

Stahl, Murray. *How They Did It: Exceptional Stories of Great Investors.* New York: Horizon Asset Management, 2011.

Duckworth, Renée A. "Catastrophes and Calms." Aeon. August 12, 2020. https://aeon.co/essays/catastrophe-drives-evolution-but-life-resides-in-the-pauses.

Deutsch, David. *The Beginning of Infinity: Explanations that Transform the World.* London: Allen Lane, 2011.

Buffett, Warren E. "Warren Buffett Joins Influencers with Andy Serwer."

Interview by Andy Serwer. Yahoo Finance, May 10, 2019. Transcript. https://finance.yahoo.com/news/influencers-transcript-warren-buffett-104802742.html.

Cassel, Ian. "Evolve or Die." MicroCapClub. October 14, 2019. https://microcapclub.com/2019/10/evolve-or-die/.

Chapter 10

Benello, Allen, Michael van Biema, and Tobias Carlisle. *Concentrated Investing: Strategies of the World's Greatest Concentrated Investors.* Hoboken, NJ: John Wiley & Sons, 2016.

Mier, Juan. "Deep Concentration: A Review of Studies Discussing Concentrated Portfolios." Lazard Asset Management. September 2017.

Stahl, Murray. "How Could Indexation Ever Be Invalidated?" Horizon Kinetics. 2017.

Murray, Nick. *Simple Wealth, Inevitable Wealth.* New York: The Nick Murray Company, Inc., 1999.

The Economist. "Active Fund Managers Hold Fewer and Fewer Stocks." March 8, 2018. https://www.economist.com/finance-and-economics/2018/03/10/active-fund-managers-hold-fewer-and-fewer-stocks.

Greenblatt, Joel. Interview by Barry Ritholtz. Masters in Business. Bloomberg Radio, April 20, 2018. Podcast, MP3 audio, 1:16:00. https://ritholtz.com/2018/04/transcript-joel-greenblatt/.

Buffett, Warren E., and Charles T. Munger. "Warren Buffett & Charlie Munger: Diversification." Recorded at the Berkshire Hathaway Annual Meeting, May 1996. Video uploaded by The Financial Review, January 11, 2019. YouTube video, 7:15. https://www.youtube.com/watch?v=ZJzu_xItNkY.

Block, Frank E. "Elements of Portfolio Construction." Financial Analysts Journal 25, no. 3 (May/June 1969): 123–129. https://doi.org/10.2469/faj.v25.n3.123.

Buffett, Warren E. "Letter to Shareholders—1979." Berkshire Hathaway Inc. March 3, 1980. https://www.berkshirehathaway.com/letters/1979.html.

Chapter 11

Freeman-Shor, Lee. *The Art of Execution: How the World's Best Investors Get It Wrong and Still Make Millions.* Petersfield, Hampshire: Harriman House, 2015.

Phelps, Thomas William. *100 to 1 in the Stock Market: A Distinguished Security*

Analyst Tells How to Make More of Your Money. New York: McGraw-Hill, 1972.

Akre Focus Fund. "Annual Report (Form N-CSR)." July 31, 2020. Filed with the U.S. Securities and Exchange Commission, September 2020. https://www.sec.gov/Archives/edgar/data/811030/000089853120000431/akre-ncsra.htm.

U.S. Department of Defense. "DoD News Briefing – Secretary Rumsfeld and Gen. Myers." News transcript, February 12, 2002. Archived April 6, 2016. https://web.archive.org/web/20160406235718/http://archive.defense.gov/Transcripts/Transcript.aspx?TranscriptID=2636.

Stahl, Murray. "An Unorthodox View of Emerging Market Investing." In Collected Commentaries and Conundrums Regarding Value Investing, 1995. New York: Horizon Asset Management, 1995.

Mayer, Christopher W. *World Right Side Up: Investing Across Six Continents.* Hoboken, NJ: John Wiley & Sons, 2012.

Sosnoff, Martin. *Train to Outslug the Market (What to Do if Unafraid).* New York: Limited Press, 2020.

Astrachan, Joseph, Josh Baron, and Rob Lachenauer. "Do Most Family Businesses Really Fail by the Third Generation?" *Harvard Business Review,* July 19, 2021. https://hbr.org/2021/07/do-most-family-businesses-really-fail-by-the-third-generation.

Baron, Josh, and Rob Lachenauer. *The Harvard Business Review Family Business Handbook: How to Build and Sustain a Successful, Enduring Enterprise.* Boston: Harvard Business Review Press, 2021.

Scott, James S., and Peter Xu. "Some Insider Sales Are Positive Signals." Financial Analysts Journal 60, no. 3 (May/June 2004): 44–51. https://doi.org/10.2469/faj.v60.n3.2620.

Muzea, George. *The Vital Few vs. the Trivial Many: Invest with the Insiders, Not the Masses.* New York: John Wiley & Sons, 2004

Block, Frank E. "Elements of Portfolio Construction." *Financial Analysts Journal 25,* no. 3 (May/June 1969): 123–129. https://doi.org/10.2469/faj.v25.n3.123.

Lynch, Peter, and John Rothchild. One Up on Wall Street: How to Use What You Already Know to Make Money in the Market. New York: Simon & Schuster, 1989.

Chapter 12

Mayer, Christopher W. *100 Baggers: Stocks that Return 100-to-1 and How to Find Them.* Laissez Faire Books, 2015.

Dennis, Felix. *How to Get Rich: One of the World's Greatest Entrepreneurs Shares His Secrets.* New York: Portfolio, 2008.

The Week. "Remembering Felix Dennis, in the Words of Those Who Worked for Him." June 22, 2014. https://theweek.com/articles/445814/remembering-felix-dennis-words-who-worked.

Greenstreet, Rosanna. "Q&A: Felix Dennis." The Guardian, May 7, 2010. https://www.theguardian.com/lifeandstyle/2010/may/08/felix-dennis-interview.

Saint-Raymond, Léa. "How to Get Rich as an Artist: The Case of Félix Ziem—Evidence from His Account Book from 1850 through 1883." Nineteenth-Century Art Worldwide 15, no. 1 (Spring 2016). https://www.19thc-artworldwide.org/spring16/saint-raymond-on-how-to-get-rich-as-an-artist-felix-ziem.

Appendix

Mauboussin, Michael J., and Dan Callahan. "Return on Invested Capital: How to Calculate ROIC and Handle Common Issues." Consilient Observer. Morgan Stanley Investment Management. October 6, 2022. https://www.morganstanley.com/im/publication/insights/articles/article_returnoninvestedcapital.

INDEX